NEW MEXICO MAVERICKS

NEW MEXICO MAVERICKS

Stories from a Fabled Past

Marc Simmons

SANTA FE

Cover Art by Ron Kil
*All photographs and illustrations
are from the author's collection unless otherwise indicated.*

© 2005 by Marc Simmons. All rights reserved.
No part of this book may be reproduced in any form or by any electronic or mechanical means including information storage and retrieval systems without permission in writing from the publisher, except by a reviewer who may quote brief passages in a review.

Sunstone books may be purchased for educational, business, or sales promotional use. For information please write: Special Markets Department, Sunstone Press, P.O. Box 2321, Santa Fe, New Mexico 87504-2321.

Library of Congress Cataloging-in-Publication Data:

Simmons, Marc.
  New Mexico mavericks : stories from a fabled past / Marc Simmons.
     p. cm.
  ISBN 0-86534-500-7 (hardcover : alk. paper) — ISBN 0-86534-467-1 (softcover : alk. paper)
 1. New Mexico—History—Anecdotes. 2. New Mexico—Biography—Anecdotes. 3. Frontier and pioneer life—New Mexico—Anecdotes. I. Title.

F796.6.S56 2005
978.9—dc22
                                              2005027362

WWW.SUNSTONEPRESS.COM
SUNSTONE PRESS / POST OFFICE BOX 2321 / SANTA FE, NM 87504-2321 /USA
(505) 988-4418 / *ORDERS ONLY* (800) 243-5644 / FAX (505) 988-1025

FOR
MELANIE,
MOLLIE
&
BEN

NEW MEXICO, USA
In 1912 a presidential proclamation made
New Mexico the 47th State of the Union.

CONTENTS

FOREWORD / 9

I
WHEN SPAIN RULED / 13

An Expedition of Lost Scoundrels / 15
Our Conquistador Poet / 19
The Well-Traveled Fray Alonso / 23
Governor Lopez and the Inquisition / 27
The Death of Governor Diego de Vargas / 31
Governor Anza's Mercy Errand, 1780 / 35
Don Pedro Buys a Carriage / 39

II
UNDER THE MEXICAN FLAG / 43

A Duel Below the Mountains / 45
The Greens of Bent's Fort / 51
An Early Glimpse of Santa Fe / 55
An Irish Artist Paints the Governor / 59
Incident at Los Valles / 63

III
FIGHTING INDIANS / 67

Chief Ecueracapa / 69
An Incident in Kiowa History / 73
Encounter With The Navajo / 77
Quanah—A Celebrated Indian / 81
Death of Cadete / 85
Battle at Monica Spring / 89
The Strange J.C. Brock / 93

IV
THE SOLDIERS' VIEW / 99

An Army Problem / 101
Major Wynkoop Recalls / 105
Soldiering in Southern New Mexico / 109
The Death of Captain Stanton / 113
When "Mary Ann" Saved The Day / 117
An Artist In Santa Fe, 1865 / 121
Captain Bourke and the Snake Dances / 125

V
MEN OF STANDING / 129

A Texan Judge in New Mexico / 131
Hang the Bishop! / 135
Governor Abeytia's Debt / 139
Senator Doolittle Tours New Mexico / 143
Strange Mr. Maxwell / 147
A German in New Mexico / 151
Doctoring in Bernalillo / 155
The Strange End Of "King Saul" / 159

VI
FOREVER, COWBOY / 163

Cowboys of the Llano / 165
A Greenhorn Makes the Grade / 169
A Teenager's Rite of Passage / 173
Those Cowboys With Ropes / 177
McJunkin Finds Some Bones / 181
The Cowboy Detective / 185

VII
ITINERANT WRITERS / 189

"Go West, Young Man" / 191
A Remarkable Newspaperman / 195
Ambling in the Southwest / 199
A Journalist's Visit to Santa Fe, 1875 / 203
A Bostonian's Prejudiced View of New Mexico / 207

VIII
WOMEN OF GUMPTION / 211

Mystery of the Blue Lady / 213
Mrs. Villalpando's Last Stand / 217
Susan Wallace Writes A Book / 221
The Indomitable Mrs. Stevenson / 225
The Remarkable Sadie / 229
Rachel Plummer's Captivity / 233
"Steamboat" at Otero / 237
Fleeing From Geronimo / 241

IX
THROUGH CHILDREN'S EYES / 245

Growing Up In New Mexico / 247
Kit's Son Goes To College / 251
A Boy's View Of Life In The Mines / 255
Billy's Boyhood / 259

FOREWORD

THERE IS SOMETHING ABOUT NEW MEXICO that has long proved attractive to mavericks, eccentrics, outsiders. I can't say precisely what it is, but it has to do with the uncommon mix of landscape, sparkling air, history, multiple cultures and isolation from America's mainstream.

Since the days of the first Spanish settlers, New Mexico has been a place where a fellow could come and spin out his own, highly individualistic pattern of living. I recall the many references I have seen in the colonial documents dealing with the complaints put forth by local officials against those pioneer New Mexicans who would not conform.

To the despair of the King's officers, they insisted upon scattering out in the remote countryside instead of congregating in neat, fortified towns as the law required. Governor Fernando de la Concha in 1788 claimed his subjects were "churlish by nature" and wanted "to live in perfect freedom" away from the regulating hands of church and state.

An escape to the wilds of New Mexico was in the minds of artists and writers two centuries later who fled the East Coast to found colonies in Santa Fe and Taos. They wanted to leave the constraints of their own society, and at the same time find a land that could stimulate creative juices.

Englishman D.H. Lawrence spoke for all of them when he exclaimed passionately, "For greatness of beauty I have never experienced anything like New Mexico."

Here, in the wide sunlit reaches at the heart of the Southwest, inspired men and women felt free to express their literary and artistic impulses. "New Mexico is like that," wrote Conrad Richter. "You never know in what obscure canyon or on what sunbaked mesa you will find an artist or scholar in exile."

In the years following World War II, word circulated in Bohemian circles throughout the country that the small and distant University of New Mexico offered a congenial atmosphere for nonconformists. To the campus came, if not a host, at least a respectable tribe of free-thinking youths. Below the shadow of the Sandia Mountains, there grew a tiny island of intellectual rebeldom.

Prominent in the ranks of this new generation of escapists was Edward Abbey. As a student, he wrote novels, finely crafted novels set in New Mexico and featuring stubborn, enduring, individualistic New Mexicans. That was in the days, of course, before he had gained a national reputation for his fiercely partisan writings on behalf of conservation.

One of Abbey's campus-born books was *Fire on the Mountain*, a novelistic treatment of the Prather episode in the Tularosa Basin. A few years before, 82-year-old rancher John Prather had grabbed headlines across the country when he took up a rifle to protect his home and land. The Army had condemned them as part of the expansion of White Sands Missile Range.

Using author's license, Abbey doctored the story a bit, both for dramatic effect and to better hammer home his message. But the book's hero, old John Vogelin, accurately mirrors the tenacity and courage of the real John Prather.

At the end, with all the forces of the establishment arrayed against him, Abbey has Vogelin utter his credo. The rancher declares: "I ain't going to give in like a gentleman. If I have to give in, I'm going to give in like an Apache. That's part of the pattern. That's the tradition around here."

The reader understands the phrase, "giving in like an Apache," to mean "going down fighting against impossible odds." And Vogelin is right. That tradition runs deep in New Mexico history, and it still possesses plenty of strength.

Across the centuries, here in the heartland of the upper Rio Grande, sturdy folk have left us a wealth of stories full of adventure, humor, tragedy, melodrama, joy and mystery. Those are the very elements that can lure readers of all ages into the world of books. Story-telling has been part of the human experience since our ancestors lived in caves. So, after all this time, we are deeply attached to the telling of tales.

As a professional historian of the old school, I remain firmly wedded to the writing of narrative history, that is, history rendered as a story with a beginning, a middle and an end.

Honest historical narrative in no way slights the quest for truth or abandons respect for authenticity in describing the past. Rather, it calls upon legitimate literary devices that help to engage and hold a readership, with the aim of building a genuine "sense of history" in a wider audience.

For more than fifty years, I have been chasing down New Mexico history and have found it to be one long excursion into high adventure. In the process, I've written hundreds of short pieces, mini-episodes as it were, concerning the people, places and events that collectively make up the richly-textured story of New Mexico.

This book pulls together a collection of some of my favorite pieces. It focuses on individuals, who in a measure large or small, left a mark on New Mexican culture and the pages of history.

I will be well-satisfied should a significant number of this book's readers come away with the desire to explore further the rewarding world of New Mexicana. It encompasses the richest body of regional history to be found anywhere within the United States.

—Marc Simmons
Cerrillos, New Mexico

I

WHEN SPAIN RULED

Spanish soldiers in 16th century dress (re-enactors)

AN EXPEDITION OF LOST SCOUNDRELS

ALL NEW MEXICANS, I feel sure, have heard of the explorer Coronado. If for no other reason, his name is on the largest shopping mall in the state, at Albuquerque.

Almost no one, however, can claim familiarity with another 16th century conquistador, Captain Francisco Leyva de Bonilla. His small-time excursion into infamy and disaster has faded from the radar screen of history.

Bonilla first surfaces in 1593 when he commanded a rough company of frontier soldiers in Nueva Vizcaya. That colonial province was centered upon the modern Mexican state of Chihuahua, bordering New Mexico.

Indians were raiding cattle ranches, so Bonilla and his troop received orders to track them down. But upon reaching the northern edge of the frontier, Captain Bonilla saw opportunity and seized it. He decided to invade New Mexico!

Several small expeditions to the upper Rio Grande had followed in the wake of Coronado's 1540 exploration. Nonetheless, New Mexico remained little known, although rumor hinted it to be rich in silver and gold.

Bonilla paused at the last outpost of Santa Barbara to gather supplies for his march northward. There an officer of the governor reached him with a warning to go no further under penalty of being condemned as a traitor to the king.

That dire threat failed to deter the errant Captain. But some of his own soldiers took heed and deserted his foolhardy enterprise. That proved wise, since not one Spaniard who accompanied the ill-fated party ever returned.

The band of outlaw fortune-hunters, for that's what they had become, made good time and soon reached the Piro pueblos in the Socorro Valley. From that point, they rapidly ascended the Rio Grande to the cluster of Tewa villages below the Sangre de Cristo Mountains.

At the Indian town that would later be called San Ildefonso, the Spaniards rudely moved in and established their headquarters. From here, they seemed to have ranged widely throughout the country looking for signs of mineral wealth.

When nothing was found, they turned their hopes eastward toward the Great Plains. Perhaps the San Ildefonso Indians wishing to be rid of them related the bogus story, given a half century earlier to Coronado, about a golden kingdom there named Quivira.

So away went the ruffians, and all the Pueblos must have breathed a sigh of relief. Unlike Coronado, Captain Bonilla and his companions came to grief on the plains of Kansas and were seen in New Mexico no more.

They found Quivira at trail's end all right, but it was nothing more than a massive village of grass houses, inhabited by Wichita Indians. The people possessed not a single ounce of treasure.

The disappointment may have sparked the falling out between Bonilla and one of his men, Antonio Gutiérrez de Humaña. Whatever the cause, Humaña stabbed his Captain with a butcher knife and killed him. He then took control of the expedition.

Shortly afterward, the Quiviran Indians attacked the camp and in a furious and bloody battle lasting most of a day, all the Spaniards were killed.

An Indian servant belonging to Humaña managed to escape and flee into the plains. But he promptly became a captive of the Apaches.

This servant, Jusepe, is the most interesting figure in the entire episode. An Aztec born near Mexico City, he had been employed long enough by Humaña to have learned Spanish.

After several years as an Apache prisoner, he heard that other Spaniards had reached New Mexico. The news led him to escape his captors and hasten west toward the Rio Grande.

At San Juan Pueblo late in 1598, he found Juan de Oñate and his colonists. He was welcomed with open arms.

Jusepe gave a formal declaration, describing what had happened to the Bonilla expedition after leaving Nueva Vizcaya. Since he was the sole survivor, it is our only source of information on the activities and fate of the party.

Iron and steel artifacts taken by the Quivirans after the massacre became scattered over the plains. Examples are occasionally plowed up today. But in almost every case they are mistakenly identified as having been "lost by Coronado." Everyone has heard of him, while few know the story of Bonilla.

Gaspar Pérez de Villagrá, New Mexico's Soldier Poet of the 17th century

OUR CONQUISTADOR POET

CAPTAIN GASPAR PÉREZ DE VILLAGRÁ published an epic poem in 1610. Written in classical style, it was fashioned in imitation of the *Aeneid* by the Roman poet Virgil. The poem bore the rather colorless name, *Historia de la Nueva México*.

Villagrá is rated by historians as one of the chief military officers serving under Governor Juan de Oñate in the founding of New Mexico beginning in 1598. He played a major role in organizing the expedition, serving as supply-master prior to its departure for the upper Rio Grande.

In some ways, Villagrá was typical of the Spanish conquistador class. He thirsted for adventure and was ambitious to acquire wealth. Most of all he wanted to leave some personal mark on history.

Born in Puebla east of Mexico City in 1555, the young man attended Spain's celebrated University of Salamanca. Juan de Oñate's twin brother Cristóbal was also a student there.

We can't help but wonder whether they became friends, leading years later to Villagrá's participation in the colonization of New Mexico.

In any case, by the time Juan de Oñate left central Mexico with soldiers and settlers, Captain Villagrá already formed part of his inner circle.

The stirring, often violent events that occurred over the next two years gave the budding poet plenty of grist for his literary mill. He was usually in the thick of the action.

For example, in late 1598 Villagrá rode alone from Isleta to report to Governor Oñate who was then at Zuni. On the way, he narrowly missed being slain by the newly hostile Acomas.

The governor's nephew and a dozen soldiers were later attacked at the pueblo and killed. In retaliation, the Spaniards destroyed Acoma.

Villagrá left the most vivid description of the furious battle. In his poem, he gives details provided by no other account.

In 1600 Governor Oñate sent his trusted captain with an escort back to Mexico to seek more supplies and men. When the party was ready to return to New Mexico, the viceroy removed Captain Villagrá from command and appointed another in his place.

Angry, Villagrá took sanctuary in a church to avoid returning, in an inferior position, to Oñate's colony. In 1605 he left for Spain, hoping to persuade the king to grant him some royal favor for his service in New Mexico.

Five years later, the captain was probably living in the university town of Alcalá de Henares east of Madrid, where his long poem *Historia de Nueva México* was published as a book. It covered the first year of Oñate's settlement.

Scholars consider the *Historia*, based on the author's eyewitness observations, to be better history than literature. Rendered in blank verse, the poem contains all sorts of literary flourishes and moral platitudes that were popular in Villagrá's day.

Still, his work, even now, makes for intriguing reading. Remarkably, it was the first printed history of any part of the United States, its 1610 publication date coming 14 years before Captain John Smith's *General History of Virginia*!

In 1992 the University of New Mexico Press republished Villagrá. The handsome volume contained both the Spanish and an English translation of the poem.

The original 1610 edition of the book had a woodcut portrait of Gaspar Pérez de Villagrá. The illustration shows a stern, elderly man, balding and wearing a thick fluted collar. He has a walrus mustache and a thick pointed beard. It is the only known image of any person in New Mexico prior to 1680.

The poem ended with the battle of Acoma. Villagrá may have intended to write a second installment, describing happenings in New Mexico up to his departure. Unhappily, he never got around to it.

Incidentally, Pérez de Villagrá finally was granted a political office in Guatemala. But on the voyage from Spain in 1620, he died and was buried at sea.

MEMORIAL

QVE FRAY IVAN DE SANTANDER DE LA

Orden de san Francisco, Comiſſario General de Indias, preſenta a la Mageſtad Catolica del Rey don Felipe QVARTO nueſtro Señor.

HECHO POR EL PADRE FRAY ALONSO de Benauides Comiſſario del Santo Oficio, y Cuſtodio que ha ſido de las Prouincias, y conuerſiones del Nueuo-Mexico.

TRATASE EN EL DE LOS TESOROS eſpirituales, y temporales, que la diuina Mageſtad ha manifeſtado en aquellas conuerſiones, y nueuos deſcubrimientos, por medio de los Padres deſta ſerafica Religion.

CON LICENCIA

En Madrid en la Imprenta Real. Año M. DC. XXX.

Title Page of Father Benavides's 1830 Memorial

THE WELL-TRAVELED FRAY ALONSO

I'VE LONG THOUGHT that among the most remarkable men of 17th century New Mexico was the ambitious Franciscan Fray Alonso de Benavides.

Today, he is remembered primarily for two things: first, his connection to the bringing of the religious statue of La Conquistadora to New Mexico in 1625; and second, his authorship of a lengthy report, or Memorial, on New Mexican affairs that he personally delivered to King Phillip IV in 1630.

In 1625, Fray Alonso, having been selected as head of the missionary program in New Mexico, started up the Camino Real from Mexico City. Toward the end of the year, his caravan passed through the string of Piro pueblos.

He would later write: "These are the first people one meets upon entering New Mexico, ... and they always assist travelers, weary from the long journey."

On January 24, 1626, Benavides reached Santa Fe. His arrival was greeted by the firing of cannons and much pomp, as all citizens turned out with the governor to welcome him.

Accompanying Benavides were twelve new Franciscans to staff outlying missions. He also brought a quantity of supplies and equipment. An inventory of these goods was translated and published in the 1940s.

One of the listed items was a small shipping box in which a carving of the Virgin was packed. Distinguished priest and historian

Fray Angelico Chávez in 1947 announced his conviction that the box had contained the Marian statue later called La Conquistadora.

Until then origins of the image had been in doubt. We knew that it was in the capital prior to the Pueblo Revolt of 1680, and had been saved, carried by fleeing colonists to El Paso and returned to Santa Fe in 1692-93.

What caused Fray Angelico to link this statue with the one Benavides imported in 1625 was the dimensions of the shipping box, provided by the priest's old inventory.

With that information in hand, he went and measured La Conquistadora, now preserved within her own side-chapel of Santa Fe's cathedral. Fray Angelico's findings revealed that the Conquistadora statue would have fit comfortably into the 1625 box, with enough space all around for protective packing.

While this and other bits of evidence were not conclusive proof, Fray Angelico thought he had enough to say that the date of the statue's arrival in New Mexico had been established. His conclusion soon won general acceptance.

Fray Alonso carried out his duties faithfully during a three-year stay in New Mexico. He got to know all of the Indian pueblos and even attempted to convert the wild Apaches living in the remote western part of the province.

In the autumn of 1629, he was recalled to Mexico City to report upon the progress of the missionary program among the Pueblos. There he was granted an audience with the viceroy, who was so impressed that he insisted on Benavides going to Spain to deliver his report to the king.

Once in Madrid, Father Benavides wrote up his account of New Mexico affairs and saw it printed, allowing him to make a formal presentation to the king.

This document is known to scholars as the Benavides Memorial of 1630. It contains much useful history, population figures for individual Pueblo villages and some unique glimpses of life along the upper Rio Grande.

In a letter from Madrid to his fellow missionaries back in New Mexico, Fray Alonso declared that his printed Memorial, given to his Majesty and advisers had been so well received that he was revising and expanding it to bring out a new edition.

Father Benavides spent several years getting the job done. On February 12, 1634 he was in Rome where he presented Pope Urban VIII with a just released copy of his Revised Memorial of 1634.

In that book, Benavides urged establishment of a bishopric in New Mexico, with its seat and cathedral to be placed at Santa Fe. For some time, he had been campaigning to be named New Mexico's first bishop, as he was eager to return to his beloved Pueblo missions.

Instead, for obscure reasons, he was appointed as the new auxiliary bishop for the Portuguese colony of Goa in India. Father Benavides is last seen in Lisbon, taking ship for the Far East.

Thereafter, he drops from the record and is thought to have died while crossing the Arabian Sea.

However, his books live on. An English translation of the 1630 Memorial appeared in 1916, while the lengthier 1634 Memorial was published in 1945. They remain valuable sources on the land and people of New Mexico in the 17th century.

Ox cart, of the kind that carried Governor López to Mexico City to face the Inquisition.

GOVERNOR LOPEZ AND THE INQUISITION

IN THE YEARS before the great Pueblo Revolt of 1680, New Mexico was torn by internal strife between two contending factions.

One party was headed by the Franciscan friars who had grown prosperous and powerful through development of their flourishing missions among the Pueblos. Their ecclesiastical capital was located at Santo Domingo, 30 miles downriver from Santa Fe.

The second faction was led by a succession of Spanish governors from Mexico City, each of whom attempted to limit the clergymen's expanding influence over New Mexico's politics and economy.

The missionaries saw themselves as protectors of the Indians. The governors, on the other hand, often exploited Pueblos and captive Apaches, to wring extra profit out of their stays in New Mexico.

One of the worst offenders was Bernardo López de Mendizábal who reigned as governor from 1659 to 1662. On entering New Mexico, the first church he reached was the mission at Socorro.

The priest there, Fray Benito, received him cordially with arches of flowers over the road and clanging of the bell in welcome. The elderly cleric, instead of thanks for his courtesy, got a severe dressing down. He was curtly informed by López that he ought to have gone out five miles on the road to meet him, as a sign of respect.

"I should be received like the Blessed Sacrament in procession, with incense," declared the arrogant official. Within a few days, everyone throughout the province had heard the story and knew they must contend with another pompous governor.

Upon assuming charge in Santa Fe, Governor López promptly sent out a military expedition to punish Apache raiders. The Franciscans charged that his aim was primarily to obtain Indian captives, which he afterward sent down the Camino Real to be sold into slavery at the silver mines.

Under Spanish law, that was strictly illegal. The accusation against the governor apparently was true.

López tried to intimidate his critics by boasting openly that he carried an order from the viceroy allowing him to hang any priest who opposed him. That preposterous claim was definitely not true!

From that point, the López administration went steadily downhill. The wonder is that it lasted as long as it did.

Father Alonso de Posada, head of the Franciscan Order in New Mexico, was also local agent for the Holy Office of the Inquisition, whose high court presided in the viceregal capital. Thus, he could gather evidence and order the arrest of persons for religious crimes.

After a formal investigation, Posada charged López de Mendizábal with heresy, blasphemy, suspicion of witchcraft, and sex crimes. In part, the blasphemy was based on the ex-governor's statement to the priest at Pecos pueblo that he, López, had higher authority than the Pope.

In all, the formal bill of indictment sent to the Holy Office contained more than 250 articles.

In August of 1662, López was arrested and his personal property confiscated. The following October, he was placed in chains and loaded in a crude ox cart for the long journey south to the Inquisition trial awaiting him.

The two-wheeled cart was very different and far less comfortable when compared to the luxury coach that first brought him to Socorro three years earlier. Throughout the trip, he could be heard loudly lamenting the injustice of his fate.

For months, the disgraced Governor López stood before the Grand Inquisitors and listened to the mountain of evidence against him. He refused to repent, maintaining that the accusations were falsehoods trumped up by the rascally clergy of New Mexico.

As the case dragged on and the strain increased, López's health began to fail. A doctor tended him in his dungeon cell, but to no avail. The former New Mexican governor died on September 16, 1664. He was buried in a corral at the Inquisition's secret prison.

Don Bernardo's story, filled with absurdities, reads like a comic opera. Nevertheless, it had grave consequences. For his misconduct, and that of other governors who disrupted colonial society, contributed directly to the catastrophic Indian revolt in 1680.

Coat of Arms of General Diego de Vargas

THE DEATH OF GOVERNOR DIEGO DE VARGAS

DON DIEGO DE VARGAS, without question, stands as the best known figure in the history of 17th century New Mexico.

He was the man who led the reconquest and re-occupation of the province in 1692-1693, in the wake of the Pueblo Revolt of 1680. Upon that rests his fame today.

In New Mexico, De Vargas held both the offices of governor and captain-general, the latter title indicating that he was commander of all military forces—regular troops and militia.

In 1696 his term as governor expired and he underwent the judicial review of his administration required of all royal officials. At that time, the Santa Fe *cabildo*, or town council, with whom he had often clashed, leveled serious charges against him, including embezzlement.

Poor De Vargas suffered the indignity of house arrest for several years, before he was able to go to Mexico City. There he launched a campaign to clear his name.

In 1702, a royal *cédula*, or decree of the King, exonerated him and extended him reappointment as governor of New Mexico. It also elevated De Vargas to the ranks of the nobility with the title of Marqués.

The governor did not arrive back in Santa Fe and assume office until November 10, 1703. Tragically for him, his term would be cut thort.

The following March reports reached De Vargas that the Faraon Apaches were continually stealing livestock from ranches in the vicinity of Bernalillo. The Faraons were the Apaches we know today as Mescaleros.

The situation convinced General De Vargas that a full-scale campaign was needed. To that end, he mustered 46 soldiers from the Santa Fe presidio and more than 100 Pueblo militiamen.

Even though he was more than 60 years old and not in the best of health, De Vargas decided to lead the operation himself. On March 27, he started downriver with his troops, accompanied by a military chaplain.

It is possible that the governor had a premonition of death. Before his departure from the capital, he took some steps to settle his affairs. On the journey south, several soldiers came down with a sickness so grave they had to be sent back to the presidio.

Once in Bernalillo, the general conducted an inspection and review of his troops. Then on March 30, he sent out Pueblo scouts to search the country for Apaches, as far as the mouth of Carnue (now Tijeras) Canyon.

De Vargas followed with his men, apparently intending to pursue the Indians until they could be cornered and engaged in battle. On April 2, however, the campaign journal he was keeping suddenly breaks off.

The reason is clear. From other documents, we learn that the next day, April 3, Governor De Vargas was stricken with high fever and acute stomach pains. Whether it was the same malady that afflicted his own soldiers a few days earlier is unknown.

He was immediately taken back to Bernalillo, probably on an improvised horse litter. There he lingered for several days, making his final confession to the chaplain and receiving the sacrament of Extreme Unction.

With strength fast waning, the governor dictated a will, naming as the executor his old friend and comrade in arms, Captain Juan Páez Hurtado.

The document provided for dispersal of his estate, including a collection of 33 books, and gave detailed instructions as to his funeral and burial inside the main church at Santa Fe.

As a marqués, governor, and captain-general, De Vargas wanted to go out in grand style. He specified that his body should lie in state before the main altar for nine days, the casket surrounded by 100 candles.

In the tradition of Spanish nobility, he also set aside money to buy 50 bushels of corn and 12 head of cattle to be distributed among Santa Fe's poor on the day of his burial.

A leading De Vargas scholar, Professor John L. Kessell, says that the governor died at Bernalillo "about sunset on the afternoon of April 8, 1704." Captain Hurtado at once sent news of his passing to government officials in Mexico City.

The following April 20, an inventory was made of the late governor's estate and was filed in the provincial archive. It is preserved today in the holdings of the New Mexico State Records Center and Archives.

Hopi Indians (engraving)

GOVERNOR ANZA'S MERCY ERRAND, 1780

ON SEPTEMBER 10, 1780 New Mexico's Governor Juan Bautista de Anza departed Santa Fe at the head of a 126 man expedition. His destination was the homeland of the Moqui Indians, known today as the Hopis.

This tribe lived in seven pueblos atop mesas in what is now northern Arizona, but was then the far reaches of western New Mexico. At the time of the great Pueblo Revolt, the Moqui had slain their three priests and burned the missions.

In the years that followed, the Spaniards tried again and again to bring these rebel Indians back under their control, using both force and peaceful persuasion. But the Moqui, led by their caciques, or religious shamans, refused to yield.

In 1775, the famous Father Escalante had traveled over from Zuni to examine conditions in the Moqui villages. He found they numbered 7,500 and were quite prosperous with their livestock and small fields.

To this day, the Hopis are celebrated for their ability to raise corn, beans, and squash on arid ground at the edge of sand dunes. They sow drought-resistant seeds deeply to take advantage of scanty moisture.

In 1777, however, a severe drought struck the Southwest and lasted for three years. The Moqui crops failed, their springs for drinking dried up, and people began to die of starvation.

To make matters worse, the tribe's arch enemies, the Navajos and the Utes, stepped up raids against the mesa-top villages.

Some desperate parents traded their small children to the Walapai who lived to the west in exchange for food. Other families packed up a few possessions and became vagabonds in search of new homes.

A few of the Moqui refugees found their way into the Rio Grande Valley and from them Governor Anza first learned of the terrible situation in their homeland.

In the disaster, he saw an opportunity. It was then that the governor organized his expedition with the double purpose of taking relief supplies to the Moqui and also using the occasion to try to persuade them to submit to King and Church.

With packmules carrying sacks of corn, Anza guided his men westward to Zuni Pueblo, the last place under Spanish rule. Drought there had also caused loss of life and he had to distribute some of the supplies meant for the Moqui.

Then he pushed on toward the Moqui villages. Some 40 hungry families heard he was coming and started forward to meet him. Tragically, they were attached by Apaches and all were massacred, except two who escaped to tell the tale.

Anza finally reached the pueblo of Oraibe, which exists to this day. He handed out corn to the first people he met and continued on until he found the village cacique.

The governor, through an interpreter, made a pretty little speech in which he urged the cacique "to accept the true God and recognize the King of Spain."

That individual replied politely that he considered the Spaniard's God to be the same as that of the Moquis, and he was satisfied with what he had. But if any of his people wished to return with Anza and become Christians, he would not object. In fact, some did go back.

Looking about, Governor Anza saw how very grim was the Moqui situation. Two of their pueblos were completely abandoned, and the remaining five were inhabited by a few hundred walking skeletons. All the rest of their once large population was either dead or scattered.

Now the people were living on a rough gruel made from ground up grass and some herbs. But even that inadequate food was in short supply.

Anza tried to give the cacique of Oraibe a packmule loaded with supplies. But he refused it, saying that tribal custom required him to respond with a gift of equal value, and he had nothing. Anza thought him filled with stiff-necked pride.

A priest accompanying the expedition wrote afterward that in his opinion the Moqui people were doomed to extinction. All the odds seemed to be against them.

Two years after Anza's visit, the tribe was afflicted with a devastating smallpox epidemic. Again Spanish observers predicted that the Moqui could not possibly survive.

But survive they did. Their numbers began to recover in the 20th century and by 1990 Hopi tribal membership had reached 10,000. When we know a bit of their troubled history, that seems truly remarkable!

Landau

DON PEDRO BUYS A CARRIAGE

DON PEDRO BAPTISTA PINO by my reckoning rates as one of the most memorable New Mexicans of the late colonial period. In 1812 he acquired a luxurious English carriage, and therein hangs a tale.

Born on the family estate at Tomé north of Belén about 1752, Pedro was one of seven brothers. Both his father and grandfather, as prosperous merchants, engaged in trade over the Camino Real.

Sometime after 1780, a mature Pedro Pino moved to Santa Fe. Historian Ralph Emerson Twitchell said that he became "the leading citizen of the capital, and in every way the superior of all in education and general intelligence."

Those advantages aided him in building his reputation and financial fortune. Don Pedro served first as a *regidor* (municipal councilman), then as *alcalde* (city mayor). At the same time, he developed a large sheep and goat ranch at Galisteo southeast of Santa Fe.

In 1810 the Spanish *córtes* (or congress) convened at the city of Cádiz in the southwestern corner of Spain. It dispatched invitations to each of the New World colonies to send a representative to participate in the work of the governing body.

At Santa Fe Don Pedro was selected as New Mexico's delegate. In October 1811 he started down the Camino Real on the first leg of his long journey to Spain. As he later told it, he paid all expenses from his own pocket.

Once in Cádiz, Don Pedro took his seat in the *córtes*. Other members were becharmed by his open manner and intellect. Hence, they nicknamed him "the Abraham of New Mexico."

During his stay in Cádiz, Pedro Pino wrote and published a small book, ***Exposition on the Province of New Mexico*** (1812). It contained a description of his homeland with pointed reference to its political, social and economic problems.

Soon after the book appeared, Don Pedro left for New Mexico. He traveled by way of Paris and London, spending time sight-seeing at each city. In the latter, he bought his carriage.

It was a beautifully appointed landau, an English conveyance with a finely crafted body and plush interior. The new owner admitted afterward that this landau had cost him a princely sum.

When Pino boarded a ship for Mexico, his bulky purchase accompanied him. It traveled, as the saying went, "in knockdown," meaning that the wheels and tongue had been removed and everything crated for shipment.

At the port of Veracruz on the Mexican Gulf coast, Don Pedro had his landau re-assembled, and after buying a team of draft mules and engaging a driver, he headed for Mexico City.

Following a brief layover in the viceregal capital, he began his climb northward up the Camino Real to Santa Fe, 1700 miles away.

The road for the initial two-thirds of the way was well-maintained and furnished with stone bridges and inns that supplied the overnight needs of travelers.

But as Don Pedro passed through arid Chihuahua and entered southern New Mexico, the poor condition of the Camino Real caused his shiny landau to take a battering.

Perhaps he recalled what had happened in the Socorro Valley to Mexican bishop Pedro Tamarón in 1760. The clergyman was heading for Albuquerque in a light carriage called a *volante*, or flyer.

As the road crossed a steep-sided arroyo, the carriage tipped over and the Bishop was flung to the ground. He only escaped serious injury by landing on top of a priest riding with him.

When Pino rolled into Santa Fe's plaza, after a three year absence, the landau caused quite a stir. Local folk gasped and stared.

According to local tradition, Don Pedro used his handsome carriage for many years and frequently invited friends to share it with him. "No one was so poor as to be refused when a seat was vacant."

It is highly doubtful that the Pino landau survives today. But if it did, what an exhibit, with its fascinating history, the antique vehicle would make!

On another note, a new translation of the *Exposition on the Province of New Mexico* was jointly published by El Rancho de las Golondrinas Museum and the University of New Mexico Press in 1995. So, that part of Pino's legacy remains accessible.

II

UNDER THE MEXICAN FLAG

A Tall Ute War Leader (After O.O. Howard)

A DUEL BELOW THE MOUNTAINS

EVERY SOCIETY FROM BIBLICAL TIMES to the present has had its heroes. Their deeds, celebrated in folksong and tale, serve to inspire young people and to connect a culture with its past.

The Spanish pioneers of New Mexico, during three centuries of colonial rule, raised up a legion of heroes. Unfortunately, most of their names and records of derring-do have been lost.

Among the few men whose story has been preserved and passed down to twentieth century listeners was Lucario Montoya. At the time of his memorable combat with a Ute chief, he was a mere stripling in his teens.

Lucario had been born and raised at the tiny frontier settlement of Cebolleta, sixty miles southwest of Santa Fe. For growing boys, times were hard there in the 1830s. Hostile Apaches, Navajos, and Utes conducted constant raids and no member of the community ever felt entirely safe.

The long and tragic list of casualties in the Montoya family was not an unusual one for Cebolleta. Lucario's parents, his grandfather and great-grandfather, two older brothers, and five uncles had all died at the hands of the Indians. More distant relatives who had suffered the same fate made up a separate tally.

Understandably, the only schooling village boys received was in the arts of war. When not hoeing in the fields or tending sheep, they played with deadly seriousness at wrestling, knife throwing, duels with wooden clubs, lariat tossing, and shooting matches using bows and arrows.

The Cebolletans possessed a few old Spanish muskets, or *escopetas*, given them by the royal governor in Santa Fe. But powder and lead were scarce, so the majority of the men became as handy with a bow as their enemies. Winter nights, they even chipped stone arrow points by the light from a corner adobe fireplace.

In the youthful contests of arms, Lucario Montoya was a star performer. He could hurl a knife and hit the mark on a tree forty feet away. His arrows flew straight and nearly always found the target.

Agile as an acrobat on horseback, it was said that once he had ridden down an antelope and roped it, an unheard of feat even for the boys of Cebolleta.

With all his skills, Lucario was not an imposing figure in appearance. In 1840, at age seventeen, he weighed less than 120 pounds.

He had a slight frame, neither tall nor very muscular, and his face, showing the first faint shadow of a beard, was drawn thin. But what he lacked in brute strength, he made up for in suppleness and endurance.

It was just at this time that the New Mexicans of Cebolleta and neighboring villages decided to take the offensive against their Indian foes. Noted fighter Manuel Chaves sounded the call.

He summoned the citizen's militia for the campaign, and Lucario's only surviving uncle was made second-in-command. Excitement ran high as the men broke out their weapons and the women packed up traveling rations.

To his unbounded delight, the boy Lucario was permitted to join the expedition. The days ahead promised excitement and danger, but being frontier bred he was fully prepared for whatever might lie in his path.

The doughty warriors rode north, passed the tall and black peak of Cabezon (famous in Navajo folklore), and then crossed a sandy plain leading to the foot of the Jemez mountains.

Colonel Chaves was in search of the Utes, bold and warlike tribesmen inhabiting the southern Rockies, who had been especially troublesome in recent months. And he found them, on the edge of the plain where scattered timber marked the first slopes of the Jemez.

The befeathered band of Utes outnumbered the New Mexicans four to one. Nevertheless, it was a fortunate interception, for evidently the Indians were marching south bent on another mission of war. Stopping them here was uppermost in the mind of every man, who thought of his unprotected loved ones left at home.

Chaves deployed his troops and ordered them to entrench in expectation of an attack. The war party, brimming with confidence, fanned out in a wide circle just out of musket range and began to shout and make taunting gestures.

The chief pranced forward on a white mustang. He was a huge fellow, well over six feet, with shoulders as broad as an ax handle. His finely tanned buckskin suit sported rows of fringes and large silver buttons that glittered in the sun.

Lucario Montoya and the other New Mexicans watched in fascination as the chief, for their benefit, put on a splendid display of horsemanship.

He dashed wildly back and forth, wheeling his mount in abrupt turns, vaulting to his feet in the saddle, and finally disappearing on the horse's off side and reappearing under its neck to unleash a stream of arrows. No doubt about it, the man was a formidable foe.

After this performance, the chief rode furiously toward the enemy line and then reined up suddenly. In Spanish he yelled, "Who dares to come out and fight me alone? Where is your greatest warrior? If he can defeat me, then my people will ride home and attack you no longer."

That ringing challenge chilled the blood of the New Mexicans. There were plenty of brave men among them, but not one who would look more than boy-size next to this Ute giant.

Before anyone else could make a move, Lucario ran up to his uncle. "Let me go," he cried. "If I die, there's none left in my family to mourn me. And if I should win with the help of San Esteban, this terrible war will be over."

"On your way then," the older man said gruffly to hide the pride he felt in his nephew. And Colonel Chaves, standing nearby, added, "Bring back the head of that fellow and I will make you an officer in this militia." And he meant it.

Lucario shook out a noose in his rope and hung it on his saddle horn. He checked the heavy knife in its sheath and counted the arrows in his quiver. Leaping on his horse, he bade a quiet goodbye to his friends, a final goodbye most of them felt sure.

When the slim challenger trotted forward, the Utes doubled up with laughter. The chief was most amused of all. He shouted, "What's the matter with you cowards, sending a child against me!"

But even before his words had stopped, Lucario in a blinding, perfectly coordinated motion had unloosed an arrow. The startled chief dodged cat-like, but even so the whistling missile took off part of his ear.

When he righted himself in the saddle, blood was streaming down the side of his face and the Ute horde had fallen deathly silent. This was going to be a serious fight after all.

The wounded giant now began to move with deliberate wariness. Thwang! He sent a feathered arrow from his own powerful bow. But the shot penetrated only empty space, for young Lucario in a flash had swung behind the protective shield of his horse.

The warring pair whirled in a circle around one another, firing arrows with amazing speed. But not one found its mark and both men soon exhausted their supply. The first phase of combat was over.

Next Lucario pulled out his rawhide lariat and swung a wide loop in the air. The chief followed suit with his own coiled rope. Again they circled menacingly.

Dodging, charging, each looked for a hole that would give him an advantage. The Indian threw his noose and missed, but Lucario's flew true and landed on his opponent's neck.

It looked like certain victory for the lad as he struck spurs to his mount. The chief, however, summoned his towering strength, jerked slack in the lariat, and slipped the hangman's loop from his head.

In a rage at last, he called to one of the Ute warriors on the sidelines to throw him a lance. "Foul! Foul!" shouted the New Mexicans. "You must fight with the weapons you carry." The chief paid no attention.

Instead he kicked his horse into a run and pointed the lance at the boy waiting on the field. Lucario Montoya sat his horse, thunderstruck. Should he flee or attack? Whipping out his knife, he made his choice.

As the two closed, Lucario rose in his stirrups, the blade poised for launching. There was a grinding crash, a boiling column of dust, and the ripping of flesh.

The vicious lance tore through Lucario's arm opening a ghastly wound and tumbling him unconscious to the ground. But the cheers that broke forth came from the ranks of the New Mexicans.

The vaunted Ute chief lay sprawled in a heap, a gleaming shaft of steel embedded in his throat. As if by magic, the army of painted warriors melted into the timber.

Gathered up gently by his companions, Lucario Montoya was revived and bandaged. Then the New Mexicans, with chins high and hearts proud, started homeward across the brown plain and rock ribbed mountains.

There must have been some among them who recalled how David had slain Goliath in a land just such as this more than two thousand years ago. Their own "David," the Ute slayer, was no less a hero in their eyes.

Restored Bent's Fort, Interior View. La Junta, Colorado

THE GREENS OF BENT'S FORT

IN 1833 THE ST. LOUIS BROTHERS Charles and William Bent began construction of a huge adobe fur trading post in southeastern Colorado. Called Bent's Fort, it was located on the north bank of the Arkansas River, astride the Santa Fe Trail.

In those days, the Arkansas formed the international boundary between the United States and the Republic of Mexico. From the walls of Bent's Fort, a man could look across the river into the province of New Mexico.

William Bent married a Cheyenne woman. So her tribe traded most of its buffalo robes and other furs at the fort. His older brother Charles established a home in Taos with his wife Ignacia Jaramillo. And he opened mercantile stores there and in Santa Fe.

From Missouri, the brothers brought out three slaves and put them to work at the fort. They were a couple, Dick and Charlotte Green, and Dick's brother Andrew.

The two men performed many tasks associated with the fort's flourishing business. One historian has suggested that they probably also served as butlers at occasional fancy banquets, given whenever people of rank passed through.

The real star of the Green family, however, was Charlotte. A large, genial woman, she ruled the fort kitchen and its Indian helpers ironhandedly. Within her own domain, no one trifled with Charlotte Green.

Throughout the southern plains and the Rocky Mountains, she gained a reputation for two accomplishments. The first was for her amazing cooking skills. One source rated her "a culinary divinity."

No fur trapper or Santa Fe Trail merchant bound for Bent's Fort failed to quicken his step as he drew near, knowing he would soon be treated to one of Charlotte's justly famous meals. The cook was best known for her pies, particularly pumpkin.

Charlotte's second talent lay in the field of entertainment. She was an able and vigorous dancer, and in great demand as a partner during wild fandangos held regularly at Bent's Fort.

Colonel Henry Inman would later describe Charlotte Green at these mountain man dances as always "the center of attention, the belle of the evening." And, he added, "She knew her worth and danced accordingly."

Indeed, Charlotte was often heard to say, "I am the only lady in the whole damn Indian country." By that she meant the only female American.

At the outbreak of the Mexican War (1846), General Stephen W. Kearny stopped briefly at the fort with his army. He was entertained at a special fandango.

After seizing Santa Fe on August 18, Kearny appointed Charles Bent as the first American civil governor. Leaving his family at Taos, Charles rode to Santa Fe and established a second residence in the old palace on the plaza. He also brought Dick Green down from the fort to fill the role of man-servant, befitting his new station as governor.

The following January, Bent went home to Taos for a visit, ignoring rumors that a rebellion was in the offing. Green was left in Santa Fe.

The morning after Charles' arrival in Taos, a mob including Indians from the pueblo stormed his house and shot him full of arrows. Upon receipt of the news in Santa Fe, an army force was dispatched northward to put down the uprising.

Dick Green, grief-stricken over the killing of his master, asked permission to accompany the troops. He was given arms and his wish granted.

The American soldiers surrounded the fortified Taos pueblo church, where the rebels had taken refuge. After chopping a hole in the nave's adobe wall, the attackers tossed in primitive grenades.

Explosions rocked the interior, but many defenders remained alive. The men outside peered into that smoking hell, but hesitated to enter. Then Dick Green, with a yell rushed in shooting. Where he led, others now followed, and the church soon fell.

Dick Green was severely wounded, but survived and was taken back to Bent's Fort. In gratitude for his heroism, William granted freedom to the Greens.

They left the fort in a wagon train headed for Missouri the following May and dropped from history's view. Colorado author Mark L. Gardner, however, tells me that Charlotte Green, alone shows up on the 1850 St. Louis census. Either the marriage had split up, or as seems more likely, Dick had died from the effects of his war wound.

What a book Charlotte's life would make, if we only had more information.

Uniforms of the Mexican Army (re-enactors)

AN EARLY GLIMPSE OF SANTA FE

IN 1914 A PROMINENT NEW MEXICAN, Francisco Perea, recorded his recollections of Santa Fe from his first visit there as a boy, 75 years before.

At that time, the winter of 1837-1838, the capital was in turmoil. The previous summer, revolutionaries in the northern village of Chimayo had fomented an insurrection that resulted in the deaths of the Mexican Governor Albino Perez and his staff. Perez had been captured, decapitated and his head used as a football by the rebels. That grim bit of horseplay terrified the residents of Santa Fe.

Downriver at Albuquerque, former Governor Manuel Armijo formed his personal army to quell the disturbance. He also fired off a letter asking that cavalry detachments from Chihuahua and Zacatecas be sent to his assistance.

Without waiting for the reinforcements, Armijo led his troops north and seized Santa Fe. Since he had stripped the Albuquerque Valley of all able-bodied men, many of them brought along their families, unwilling to leave them home at the mercy of hostile Indians.

It was for that reason that eight year old Francisco Perea found himself transported from Bernalillo and the spacious adobe house of his father to the hubbub of the provincial capital. He was to remain there for many months while the drama of the insurrection played itself out. In the interval, he had as much excitement as any boy could crave.

Francisco was in the streets with other citizens when shortly the cavalry from Mexico arrived. He must have been wide-eyed as the soldiers, all aglitter in their resplendent uniforms, paraded into the plaza.

With the new force added to his own, Armijo marched northward to mop up the last rebel holdouts. Word soon filtered back of his success. Then, the Governor returned with four of the enemy leaders as prisoners.

A great crowd, with young Francisco in its midst, assembled at La Garita, two blocks north of the plaza, to see what would happen. La Garita was an adobe defensive tower built on a small hill and used not only for a lookout post but as a place to execute criminals.

Manuel Armijo believed in swift and stern punishment. There was no show of a trial. The captives were stood against a wall and shot, while Francisco Perea and others looked on, tight-lipped.

For a youngster, Santa Fe was then a fascinating place, even apart form the comings and goings of soldiers and the slaying of revolutionaries. Throughout the town there was noise and movement and color.

"Upon our arrival at the capital," wrote Perea afterward, "we found it full of soldiers, citizens, and a miscellaneous gathering of humanity of all stations of life. The plaza was crowded with all kinds of vehicles, together with teamsters, camp cooks, roustabouts, horses, mules, burros, pigs and goats."

In the center of the plaza, the boy noted three cottonwoods and, directly opposite the adobe Governors Palace, a tall flagpole, "from the top of which was displayed the Mexican flag in all its glory." As a reminder of the recent turmoil, a small caliber cannon was positioned at each of the four corners of the square.

Recalled Francisco Perea, "The plaza was then a dirty, unsightly place almost to a degree unbelievable. In fact the public square, which is now a scene of beauty, was, in the years 1837 and

1838, totally destitute, and the people seemed to be satisfied with those conditions."

What particularly excited the young Perea was the monthly arrival and departure of the mail couriers. The mail pouches were carried by Pueblo Indian runners who traveled the dangerous valley road to El Paso, keeping a wary eye out for hostile Apaches.

The sum total of mail was usually a few letters and newspapers and several magazines published in Mexico City and Madrid. Subscriber of the magazines was Manuel Alvarez, a native of Barcelona who was serving as the U.S. consul in Santa Fe.

Besides watching the mail runners, a youth could find plenty else to engage his attention. Open-air gambling of all kinds went on constantly. There were games of monte, using a full deck of Spanish cards, and three-card monte, involving a sleight-of-hand performance on the part of the dealer. The roulette wheel abounded. And as Perea remembered it, "the money bet scarcely ever came back to the unfortunate dupe that 'laid it on the wheel.'"

Going busted at the games, a person could forget his woes at a cock fight, a wild Saturday night fandango, a saloon, or event at a theatrical performance of one of Cervantes' plays.

Fearing that his description of Santa Fe's social life might leave the wrong impression, the mature Francisco Perea hastened to close his recollections with a salute to the more sober and upright citizenry. "When not at work," he declared, "they were noted for their attachment to home and family and did not idle away their time on the plaza and on the streets about town."

"Time sweeps over all and covers much from sight and remembrance," he concluded, "except a few scattered items that chance to lodge in the lively brain of the individual who happened to witness them." The scattered bits Perea preserved provide us a tiny glimpse of life in New Mexico when it belonged to the Mexican Republic.

Governor Manuel Armijo, Portrait by artist Alfred Waugh

AN IRISH ARTIST PAINTS THE GOVERNOR

SOME TWENTY YEARS AGO, I received a letter from my friend, Dr. Ward Alan Minge, the noted historian who had restored and authentically furnished an historic hacienda at Corrales, north of Albuquerque. It suggested I stop by at my convenience to view an important artifact he'd recently obtained.

Several weeks later, I went to Corrales and Dr. Minge led me to his library. There he showed me a framed, unsigned portrait of a man in full dress military uniform, wearing a plumed hat and sword.

"Do you know who that is?" he asked eagerly.

"It's probably New Mexican General Manuel Armijo, our last governor under the Republic of Mexico," I guessed. The figure was quite portly, and Armijo was reported to be stout.

Minge had expected to stump me and was disappointed that I had identified his treasure so quickly. "Where did you get it?" I inquired.

It seems the picture had been in the hands of Armijo descendants, it had come up for sale, and Dr. Minge had been able to make the purchase. Beyond that he knew nothing else.

I stunned him again by saying, "I can tell you who the artist was, when he painted it, and under what circumstances." And I added that I had never expected to see the original.

The man responsible for the portrait was Irish-born immigrant Alfred S. Waugh, perhaps the first professional artist ever to visit New Mexico. In June 1846, he left Independence, Missouri headed for Santa Fe with the intention of making sketches and keeping a journal of his adventures for possible publication.

Arriving in the capital during the fiesta of St. John the Baptist, June 24, Waugh was astonished to find "the whole town alive with mirth and jollity." Gambling, cock fights, and horse racing reigned.

Governor Manuel Armijo, whom the Irish visitor called "an absolute monarch," dwelled in an adobe Palacio on the dusty square.

On Sundays, related Waugh, "the governor walks to church accompanied by his staff and followed by a military brass band composed of two very antiquated trumpets and a couple of drums."

The morning after his arrival, the artist presented himself at El Palacio for an interview with Armijo. "I arranged with his Excellency to make his likeness for my own collection."

When finished, Waugh described it as a cabinet size picture of a full length figure in uniform, with a medal on his chest and a sword at his side, which had been presented to him by the people of Chihuahua.

Armijo was so pleased with the result that he insisted that a duplicate be painted for his family. Observed Waugh, "He said I was the only artist who ever made his likeness." The duplicate was the portrait purchased 130 years later by Dr. Minge.

In 1851 Alfred Waugh in St. Louis would tell a friend that the Armijo image in his possession "as a work of art is nothing." In truth, it had little artistic merit, as he himself realized.

Its only value, Waugh soberly admitted, was historical, being a likeness of "the monarch" just before he was toppled from his throne and fled to Mexico at the outbreak of the Mexican War.

Later, Manuel Armijo would return to the new American territory and establish his residence at Lemitar, north of Socorro. There he died in 1853.

Waugh's own Armijo portrait, sketches, and most of his journal, including the account of his trip over the Santa Fe Trail have disappeared. A journal fragment and a few other papers of his are in the archive of the Missouri Historical Society, St. Louis.

When I visited Dr. Minge, he graciously allowed me to photograph the portrait. The Albuquerque Museum later acquired it, along with the entire Minge collection of Hispanic material and the hacienda, which are now available for public viewing.

Ruins today of Los Valles, destroyed in 1847

INCIDENT AT LOS VALLES

THE GHOSTLY RUINS of the once prosperous little village of Los Valles lie forgotten in the deep canyon of the Gallinas River, a dozen miles southeast of Las Vegas, New Mexico.

Several years ago I visited the site for the first time, accompanied by Professor Adrian Bustamante who was then a dean at Santa Fe Community College. We were both familiar with the tragic events that led to the destruction of Los Valles in early July of 1847.

As the two of us prowled among the walls of roofless stone buildings, we found remains of burned *vigas* (beams). They served as grim reminders of the village's fate.

How and why Los Valles was extinguished, by an attack of American forces during the Mexican War, forms only a short chapter in our history. It is one scarcely remembered today.

Events leading up to the tragedy began on August 18, 1846. On that date General Stephen W. Kearny's Army of the West, having marched over the Santa Fe Trail, seized the capital without a fight.

The U.S. flag then replaced that of Mexico throughout the territory. The downriver towns from Bernalillo to Socorro accepted the change with good grace. But in northern New Mexico hostility simmered below the surface.

On January 19, 1847 a bloody revolt occurred at Taos. Slain were newly appointed Governor Charles Bent and other local officials. The violence then spilled over the east slope of the mountains.

Near Mora local residents captured and killed several prominent merchants from Missouri. Soldiers attacked the town but were repulsed in a full scale battle. The commander, Captain Israel Hendley fell mortally wounded. A second and larger force returned with artillery and reduced Mora to rubble.

Roaming parties of lawless men continued to cause disturbances through early spring. On May 20 Major Benjamin Edmonson in command of Missouri Volunteers took up quarters in Las Vegas.

In the last week of June, raiders drove off part of the Volunteers' horseherd, grazing just outside of Las Vegas. Major Edmonson ordered Lieutenant Robert Brown, with Privates McClanahan and Quisenbury, and a native New Mexican scout, to follow the trail in an attempt to identify the culprits.

They did not return and Edmonson feared the worst. On July 5 word was received that the three soldiers and the civilian guide had found the missing government horses in corrals at Los Valles.

When the men attempted to reclaim the animals, the residents of the village rose up and killed all four of them. The news prompted the Major to take swift action.

He mustered a mobile force of 29 mounted troops and 33 infantry, plus a small piece of artillery. These he led down the Gallinas to confront the people of Los Valles.

Arriving there, Edmonson divided his unit in two and charged the village from both sides. Some 12 defenders fell in the streets and another 50 or so were captured.

A house by house search turned up clothing, weapons, and other possessions of the slain Lieutenant Brown and his men. The lieutenant's body had been tossed into some nearby boulders, while the other corpses had been burned.

By questioning prisoners, it was learned that Brown had been wearing a cross around his neck. For that reason, he was not cremated with the rest.

Since the evidence confirmed that Los Valles as a whole was guilty of the horse thefts and the killings, Major Edmonson ordered the entire community burned. The only exceptions were several houses spared to shelter women and children.

On the return trip to Las Vegas, the soldiers burned down a *molino* or gristmill belonging to the mayor of Las Vegas, Juan Maes. He was thought to have had a hand in the Los Valles violence. However, his innocence was later established, too late to save his mill.

The prisoners were sent to Santa Fe where they were tried by a court martial. Six were found guilty of capital crimes and hanged on August 3.

The site of Los Valles was apparently abandoned after its terrible ordeal. Originally, the full name of the community had been Los Valles de San Agustín.

Afterward some of the surviving inhabitants re-gathered and moved downstream a half mile. On a small flat they formed a new village, called simply San Agustín.

That place still exists. For a span of years, 1918-1966, it even had a U.S. Post Office.

III

FIGHTING INDIANS

Comanche Camp (National Archives photo)

CHIEF ECUERACAPA

THE NAMES OF SITTING BULL, Geronimo, Red Cloud, Roman Nose, Crazy Horse, Cochise, and Sequoyah are practically household words, known to everyone who is familiar with American history.

But on no list of celebrated Indian leaders will you find mention of Chief Ecueracapa. That's because he has been overlooked by history. I can only count that a grave injustice, since by all accounts this individual was one of the most remarkable figures of his time.

Indeed, I would go so far as to say that Ecueracapa, head chief of the Comanches, was the Gorbachev of his people, turning them in a new direction and changing the course of their history.

He first surfaces in 1785. At that moment, the Comanches were divided among themselves over what course to follow with regards to the Spaniards settled in New Mexico. For years they had sent their war parties to raid the towns and ranches along the Rio Grande.

Then in 1779 Governor Juan Bautista de Anza had marched out of Santa Fe with a large force. In eastern Colorado, he ambushed a main Comanche camp and killed the premier war chief Cuerno Verde and all his sub-chiefs. It was a devastating blow.

At once a peace faction formed within the tribe and attempted to arrange an end to the hostilities. But Anza refused to deal until all the Indians agreed to put down their weapons together.

An internal struggle went on for several years. But in late 1785 the peace-seekers murdered the head of the war faction, Chief Toroblanco, clearing the way for serious negotiations with the Spaniards.

It was at this point that Ecueracapa emerged from the shadows as the leading Comanche spokesman. Shortly, warriors brought a captive into camp—a Pueblo Indian from Taos who had been buffalo hunting on the plains and gotten lost.

He was fed and clothed by Ecueracapa and afterward released to carry word to Anza that the Comanches were now united and ready to make a treaty.

The governor was delighted. Immediately, he sent an invitation to Ecueracapa to come to Santa Fe, and the chief responded. Upon meeting the two gave one another an abrazo in the Spanish manner.

Anza described his guest as being "trustworthy and highly intelligent." His name Ecueracapa meant "leather jacket," and came from his habit of wearing a heavy hide vest as protection from arrows.

In Texas, where in the past the chief had gone on raids, he was known by the name Cota de Malla (Coat of Mail) because he had shown up there attired in a cast off piece of Spanish armor.

A few weeks after their get-acquainted session in Santa Fe, Anza and Ecueracapa met again at Pecos Pueblo near the edge of the plains and formalized a permanent peace treaty. The Indians buried their weapons in a hole, symbolizing the end of their war with the New Mexicans.

Besides accepting peace, the Comanches pledged to move their villages close to the settlements, carry on trade, help the Spaniards in their continuing war with the Apaches, and turn over the sons of principal chiefs to be educated by the Spaniards.

Anza's military superior in Chihuahua City approved all this and authorized the giving of a silver peace medallion and a brilliant red cape to Ecueracapa. He further promoted the chief to the rank of general with a yearly salary of 200 pesos, to be paid in trade goods.

Surprisingly, the treaty held for several decades, bringing New Mexico its first long period of peace. The success of the agreement rested largely upon Ecueracapa's sincere desire to see it work.

On numerous occasions he led his warriors against the Apaches, in fulfillment of his pledge. In 1792, for instance, he launched a 500-man campaign down the Pecos River. On the slopes of the Sierra Blanca, near the future Ruidoso, he attacked a large Apache camp and seized many horses and captives.

A short time later, he led a war party against the Comanches' traditional enemies, the Pawnees. In that episode, Ecueracapa suffered a grave wound. His men carried him back to his tepee and word was rushed to Santa Fe.

So serious was this news, the governor put the military surgeon, the only trained doctor in New Mexico, on a fast horse for the Comanche camp. But he arrived too late. The chief had died and the New Mexicans had lost their staunchest friends among the Indians.

The Spanish documents reveal quite a bit about Ecueracapa's last years. I suppose the story, when pieced together, would make a fascinating little book.

A Kiowa Boy

AN INCIDENT IN KIOWA HISTORY

THE KIOWAS WERE ONE of the smallest of the Plains Indian tribes, numbering only about 1,000 people in 1780. But by way of compensation for their small population, they displayed in war unbounded courage and ferocity.

On the frontier, it was said that the Kiowas killed more white men in proportion to their numbers than warriors of any other tribe. The historical record seems to bear out that claim.

Today, these people are best known through the writings of celebrated Kiowa author N. Scott Momaday, who grew up at New Mexico's Jemez Pueblo where his parents were teachers. Beginning with his Pulitzer Prize-winning novel, *House Made of Dawn* (1969), Momaday's books explore Kiowa history and identity.

The Kiowas first appear in the record about 1700, living on the Yellowstone River in Montana. Then they drifted south until they bumped into the Comanches of the Texas Panhandle.

The two tribes fought a short but bitter war, made peace, and thereafter remained firm friends and allies. In 1786, the Comanches formed an alliance with the Spaniards of New Mexico, but the Kiowas refused to join in and for years thereafter continued to raid the Rio Grande settlements.

One of those raids, in 1839, entered into tribal lore because of curious circumstances associated with it. At that period, all the Southwest, except for Texas, still belonged to the Republic of Mexico.

In late spring, the traditional beginning of the Indians' war season, 20 Kiowas under a leader named Painted Red departed on a raid. They meant to steal horses from the Pa'suñkos, which was the pronunciation in their own language for Paseños, or the Mexicans of El Paso.

The war party angled southwestwardly over the plains, crossed the mountains into the Rio Grande Valley, and approached the limits of El Paso at night. Much to the warriors' surprise, they found the horseherds all heavily guarded by Mexican soldiers.

Painted Red called a council. Each man had his say and it was agreed, via native democracy, to abandon the raid as too risky and to head back for the home camp.

The party rode northeast about thirty miles and stopped to rest at a famous trail landmark known as Hueco Tanks, located not far below the present-day New Mexico state line. The tanks are large natural cisterns formed by depressions in limestone.

The Kiowas paused here to drink and rest. But the delay gave a troop of soldiers who had been following the opportunity to catch up and surround them. The first volley from Mexican muskets killed several Indian horses.

Painted Red and his men found refuge in a cave. They were temporarily safe from their enemies, but neither could they escape, or so it first seemed.

The Mexican troops who went into camp within sight of the cave entrance were guided by several Mescalero Apache scouts. One of those who spoke Comanche was told to yell at the Kiowas, since they understood that language, and tell them to surrender. As his words could not be interpreted by the Mexicans, the Apache instead encouraged the entrapped warriors and urged them to hold out.

The Kiowas found themselves without food or water. So at night they had to crawl out to one of the near cisterns for a hasty drink.

At the same time, they cut strips of meat from their dead horses. But by the third day of the siege, the horseflesh had putrified. By then they were suffering terribly and knew they must escape or perish.

Now one of them noticed that a juniper tree grew on a ledge above the cave entrance, some of its roots growing down to within a few feet above the opening. Climbing these roots in the pitch dark, they determined, offered a pathway to freedom.

That night the Kiowas made it to the top, but in dislodging rocks had been fired upon and one of their prize fighting men, Koñate, was wounded. After stealing some of the army horses, they tied Koñate upon one and sped toward home.

A few days later, the Kiowas reached a familiar spring on the edge of the Great Plains. By then, Koñate appeared close to death from his wound. Therefore, his companions built an arbor of branches to shield him from the sun and left him next to the water. Upon reaching camp, they would send another party to bring back his bones for burial.

Two days afterward, the returning warriors met six Comanches headed toward Mexico. They told their story and asked their allies to stop at the spring and put rocks over Koñate's body to keep off wolves.

Imagine the surprise of the Comanches upon reaching the spring to discover Koñate alive and recovering. Promptly, they abandoned their raid and stayed to feed and nurse him.

Subsequently, the Comanches rode triumphantly into the Kiowa village and delivered Koñate to his family and tribe. He recovered fully, lived for many years, and was believed by the Kiowas, as a result, to possess supernatural powers.

Navajo With Shield and Lance (After O.O. Howard)

AN ENCOUNTER WITH THE NAVAJO

IN THE DAYS OF THE MEXICAN REPUBLIC, after 1821, the people of New Mexico waged a long and bitter war against the Navajo tribe. Which side had started the conflict, no one could say.

The Navajo Indians, for their part, made monthly raids on the Rio Grande settlements, running off flocks of sheep and carrying away women and children as prisoners. But the New Mexicans also fed the flames of war by launching regular attacks on isolated Navajo camps. Their purpose was to take captives which could be sold at 500 pesos apiece to wealthy residents of Santa Fe, Albuquerque, and El Paso.

Under Spain and later under Mexico, the holding of Indian slaves was strictly forbidden. But the New Mexicans got around the law by calling their captives *criados*, or servants.

Amado Chavez, a prominent New Mexican of the nineteenth century, described the system as he witnessed it. "On arriving home from a slaving expedition, the first thing you did was take the children to a priest to baptize them and give them a name. They would naturally take your name and as they grew up, they would consider you and your wife as their parents. If you did not have the pluck to go after Indian children yourself, you could easily buy one. It must be remembered that many parties that went after servants never returned. The Indians killed them all."

Slave-raiding, in fact, was so dangerous that most people had no stomach for it. As a result, men of the frontier village of Cebolleta west of Albuquerque came to specialize in the seizing and selling of captives. Thus, when a rich father in the Rio Grande Valley was making plans for his daughter's wedding, he would place an order with the Cebolleteños—for a Navajo boy or girl that he could present as a bridal gift.

In the 1840s the leader of the Cebolleta raiders was Redondo Gallegos, a fearless man of towering physical strength. The Navajo knew and feared him and regarded him as a worthy foe.

Once a party of ranchers from the valley below Albuquerque rode into Cebolleta. They were led by a pompous fellow named José Largo. With a tone of arrogance, he announced to the villagers that his men were tired of paying the Cebolleteños' price for servants. They were going on a raid of their own. If anyone wished to tag along and observe how real men did the job, they were welcome.

Redondo Gallegos listened quietly to this speech, noting the swagger in Señor Largo's manner. Yes, he would go. And so would 20 or so other men of the village. Being poor country bumpkins, surely they had much to learn from this army of fancy-dressed ranchers.

José Largo and his men swung out on the trail westward. They were in a festive mood, talking loudly and joking, all confident that they would soon have a valuable string of captives in tow.

Some distance behind, Redondo Gallegos and his veterans rode in subdued silence. Unlike the noisy novices in the lead, they were fully aware of the perils involved in this dangerous business.

Unexpectedly the New Mexicans came over a rise and bumped headlong into a Navajo war party, numbering perhaps a hundred warriors. Each side was seemingly as surprised as the other at the suddenness of the encounter, but it was the Indians who recovered first. They kneed their ponies forward, yelling and swinging deadly-looking clubs.

The valley ranchers, bent upon attacking small camps, had not bargained for anything quite like this. José Largo took one look at the yelling horde and broke for the shelter of some nearby timber.

The Cebolleteños, trailing far to the rear, saw their companions in wild flight with the Navajos pressing close. Accustomed to independent combat, they dashed forward and each man, following the example of Redondo Gallegos, hurled himself against the war party. They fought like enraged bobcats.

Now it was the Indians' turn to give way. On seeing the ranchers flee, they had sensed an easy victory. But then, with the appearance of their old enemies from Cebolleta, the tide turned.

Redondo Gallegos spurred up to the war chief, grabbed him by the hair, and dragged him to the ground where they grappled. As the battle parted around them, a break in the boiling dust cloud revealed that the Indian had been overcome and tied up as tightly as a wild cow. When the warriors observed the fall of their leader, they broke off the fight and melted away to the west.

Seeing the Indians depart, the ranchers came out of the woods. Their faces were well-marked with scratches from branches that had gotten in the way of their hasty flight. But even now, José Largo had not lost his insolence.

Trotting up to Redondo Gallegos, he inquired with haughtiness, "What's the matter with that Navajo lying there that you didn't promptly send him to the next world? Are you lacking in valor?"

A faint smile appeared on Gallegos' lips as he said, "You arrive a little late, Señor Largo. And you have little to teach about valor, for it seems I have the captive you were going to take. But if you wish to demonstrate your bravery, then I'll let you kill this enemy yourself. On this condition: he must be set loose and given his own bow and club. Then you two proud warriors can battle to the death."

José Largo was stunned. "That Indian is husky and mean," he whined. "If we turn him loose he'll hurt somebody. Trussed up like that, it's easy to finish him off at no risk."

"I suppose there was no risk when I captured him," Gallegos replied angrily. "But to show what Cebolleteños are made of, I'll accept this challenge myself. And I'll do so armed only with a club and my own poncho. Then maybe Señor Largo will learn something about fighting."

And so the matter was arranged. The Navajo was released and one of the men who spoke his language explained that Redondo Gallegos challenged him to personal combat.

The Indian understood perfectly. As soon as his bow and quiver were returned, he snatched an arrow, fitted it to the string and aimed at his captor's chest. Gallegos, however, had rolled the poncho on his arm, leaving a portion swinging free. As the arrow was released he dodged aside, catching it in the folds of his garment. Almost in the same movement, he made a swift lunge and felled his opponent with the club.

There was none among the ranchers now who could doubt the courage or fighting skill of Redondo Gallegos. In some haste they and their shamed leader turned homeward. And the episode, told and retold around winter fires, became part of the folklore of the village of Cebolleta.

QUANAH—A CELEBRATED INDIAN

ON MAY 6, 1892 A LAS CRUCES NEWSPAPER, *The Republican*, published the following notice: "Quanah Parker, principal chief of the Comanches from the Indian Territory, was in the city this week.

"He was on his way to the Mescalero agency (near Alamogordo) where some of his race reside. Chief Parker is wealthy, has his coach and four horses with a whiteman for coachman, and maintains great state.

"He comes dressed in broadcloth, his long black hair braided and surmounted with a silk tie, but it is said that when out on the reservation, he can appear in full Indian dress with a breech cloth."

Quanah Parker was indeed an imposing figure and he must have attracted a great deal of attention in riding through the dusty streets of Las Cruces.

His personal history is the stuff of legend. It begins with an 1836 raid the Comanches made on Fort Parker in east Texas. They killed a number of the defenders and carried several women and children into captivity.

One of the prisoners was nine year old Cynthia Ann Parker. A few years after her abduction, she married Chief Nocona, the man who had captured her. By him she had two sons, Quanah and Pecos, and much later a daughter named Prairie Flower.

Quanah Parker, Comanche Chief

Ironically, Quanah, although half white, grew up to be a prominent war leader as well as the last great chief of the Comanches.

After Nocona's band devastated several north Texas villages in 1860, Texas Rangers under Captain Sul Ross were sent in pursuit. The trail led to the Pease River in the eastern Panhandle.

The Rangers made a surprise attack on the Comanche camp and Chief Nocona was reportedly killed. His eldest son Quanah was one of the few to escape.

Among the prisoners, Captain Ross was astonished to find a woman with light skin and blue eyes. She wailed frightfully for her fallen husband and sons, whom she believed to be dead. The Texans had no idea who she was.

They took her to Fort Worth with her two year old daughter, Prairie Flower. Newspaper stories brought Colonel Isaac Parker who interviewed the woman through a Comanche interpreter.

At first the Colonel could learn little, but then he began describing the raid on Fort Parker, 24 years before, which he had survived. He mentioned that his niece Cynthia Ann had been carried away.

Recognition flooded the eyes of the captive and she suddenly exclaimed, "Cincee Ann. Me, Cincee Ann. Me Cincee Ann!" The mystery of her identity was solved.

Colonel Parker took his niece and her daughter to live with relatives, but she was never able to re-adjust to white society. She kept trying to run away and rejoin the Comanches. Well-meaning kin locked her in a cabin at night.

At age five, Prairie Flower died. Cynthia Ann never recovered from grief, and she herself succumbed from self-induced starvation in 1870.

Far to the west on the plains of Texas and eastern New Mexico, the last free Comanches were desperately hanging on to their crumbling tribal life. During the 1860s, Quanah had emerged as the principal chief.

It was reported that in those years he ordered his warriors to kill no more women and children. He had learned that his mother and little sister were living among the whites and he didn't want to take a chance of them being slain.

At the Battle of Adobe Walls, near today's Amarillo, Quanah rode at the head of 700 Comanches, Kiowas, and Cheyennes in a furious attack on a band of buffalo hunters. The Indians were driven off, the defeat leaving them badly shaken.

Soon afterward army troops came pelting after them, and in the Red River War, the southern Plains tribes were finally vanquished.

By 1875 Quanah and his people found themselves on an Oklahoma reservation, beginning a new life. During the rocky transition, Quanah continued to provide strong leadership for the tribe. But although half white, he never showed interest in Christianity or formal education.

Economically, however, he prospered as indicated by the fine clothes he was wearing when he arrived at Las Cruces in 1892, riding in his own horse-drawn coach.

Chief Quanah Parker died in 1911. He left many descendants (having been a polygamist with seven wives), and also left a lasting bond with the Comanche people.

DEATH OF CADETE

IN 1856 THE OLD MESCALERO APACHE CHIEF Barranquito died and was succeeded by his son Cadete. The father had been something of a terror on the war trail, but Cadete proved just the opposite, turning his people toward the peace road.

Long-time El Paso historian C.L. Sonnichsen called Cadete a great Apache and credits his diplomacy with averting numerous disasters that otherwise would have been the lot of the Mescaleros.

Several books mention that Cadete was murdered in La Luz Canyon near Tularosa in 1872. The circumstances of his death, however, are not generally known. I've managed to piece together the story from contemporary accounts.

It seems that in early November of that year, the Apache agent, a Mr. Curtis, asked Cadete to ride to Las Cruces to serve as a witness before a grand jury. That body was engaged in handing down indictments against non-Indians who had been selling whiskey illegally to the Mescaleros.

Cadete gladly complied. With the agency interpreter, a man named Juan Cojo, he saddled his best horse and headed for Las Cruces. There he gave the desired testimony and the pair started for home, skirting the White Sands.

That was the last either man was ever seen alive. Apparently, they reached the settlement of La Luz at the foot of the Sacramento Mountains and not far beyond were struck down by disaster.

An Apache War Leader (National Archives photograph)

A Mescalero from the agency, scouting the trail, discovered Cadete's body. Nearby was the dead carcass of interpreter Juan Cojo's horse.

The Indian went straight to Fort Stanton and reported the crime. At once, a troop of soldiers and Agent Curtis hurried to the scene to investigate. A trail of blood was seen leading from La Luz. And Cadete's pistol was found with two shots fired.

The immediate suspicion was that whiskey runners against whom Cadete testified in Las Cruces had followed him for purposes of revenge.

According to the territorial press, "Nothing has been heard from the interpreter and it is feared that he, too, has been foully murdered."

Newspapers around New Mexico lamented the loss of the chief. Said one, "There is great sorrow manifested by all citizens who knew Cadete. He had won the confidence and esteem of all."

There was serious concern also that the bloody incident might spark an Apache uprising. There was said to be great excitement on the reservation and tribesmen were reported to be cutting their hair as a sign of mourning.

Panic spread along the eastern edge of the White Sands. La Luz was totally abandoned and outlying ranchers took their families and fled to Tularosa.

The concern, nevertheless, was misplaced for the Indians remained quiet. In a few days, people of the area decided all was safe and they began a return to their homes.

Almost three weeks passed and then word was received at Fort Stanton that the remains of Juan Cojo had been located almost 20 miles from the place where Cadete had been killed. An investigative team from Fort Stanton quickly traveled to the site.

Cojo's body had been partially eaten by wolves. But enough remained to show that he had died from repeated knife wounds. That bit of evidence was enough to provide a solution to the mystery.

With Cadete had been discovered a blood-stained butcher knife. So, now it was suddenly clear that the two men were responsible for each other's deaths and no outside parties had been involved.

The best guess was that, as a result of an argument, Juan Cojo had snatched Cadete's pistol from him and shot the chief. Cadete, only wounded, went at his assailant with the knife and in the brawl recovered his pistol with which he shot and killed Cojo's horse. The interpreter, bleeding profusely, had started out on foot and made 20 miles before he dropped dead.

That reasonable explanation was apparently sufficient to satisfy the Apaches. They were reported to be calm and in no way disposed to cause trouble over the incident.

A paper in Santa Fe went so far as to say, "For Indians, they have conducted themselves admirably. In fact, no tribe could have done better under the circumstances."

BATTLE AT MONICA SPRING

THE TURMOIL AND VIOLENCE that plagued our state during 300 years of its history is now largely forgotten. So too is the courage and fortitude of those early-day New Mexicans.

A little known fight between settlers and Navajos that occurred in 1863 underscores my point. The episode can remind us at what cost New Mexico was brought into the modern world.

A chief player in the story was Manuel A. Chaves, who until the late 1850s lived at Santa Fe, in a home behind the Santuario de Guadalupe. Upon selling his residence there, he moved with his family down to the old Tomé Land Grant east of Belen and developed a large ranch.

Chaves was a seasoned Indian campaigner, and he also fought for the Union in New Mexico's Civil War battles of Valverde and Glorieta. Afterward, returning to his ranch he found that Indians had stripped it of several thousand head of livestock.

One morning a messenger reached him with an urgent appeal for aid. A hundred Navajos had struck ranches in the upper Socorro Valley, seizing stock and carrying off the young son of distinguished citizen Matías Contreras.

Manuel Chaves at once gathered eight of his own men and rode to the Contreras hacienda where they were joined by another rancher, Don Tomás Baca, and his four vaqueros. A rider was sent to Fort Craig for reinforcements, but Matías Contreras, distraught

Manuel A. Chaves, Fought the Navajos at Monica Spring

over the loss of his son, insisted that they start the pursuit without waiting for the soldiers.

Owing to his experience, Chaves assumed command and led the men westward around the Magdalena Mountains and then turned south to the foothills of the San Mateos.

Following the broad livestock trail, they soon ran into the Navajo rear guard near Monica Spring.

Manuel had probably been hoping that their sudden appearance would startle the raiders, causing them to abandon the stolen stock and flee. Instead, the Navajos, seeing they had their foes outnumbered, turned around to give battle.

Grasping the seriousness of the situation, Chaves dismounted his men, had them tie their saddle mules in the rear, and take cover in some stunted junipers. But Navajo sharpshooters flanked their position and in a few minutes shot down all the mules.

For the rest of the day, the normal serenity of Monica Spring was disrupted by the steady sound of gunfire. The New Mexicans were fighting for their lives, and given the odds, it seemed that all were surely doomed.

Manuel slipped from man to man bolstering their courage and occasionally, because of his superior marksmanship, firing their rifles while they loaded his single-shot Hawken. A red tie around his neck made him a conspicuous target, but in spite of pleas from his comrades, he refused to remove it.

His foreman José Chaves had suffered several wounds, yet he bravely kept shooting and reloading. Finally he dropped with a bullet through his head. By nightfall only Manual Chaves, Tomás Baca, and Matías Contreras were left.

Baca had received a severe wound that shattered his lower leg. Under cover of darkness, his two companions dragged him to a sheltered spot on a hillside. They could easily have abandoned him and escaped, but that was not even considered.

Manuel had only three bullets remaining in his shot pouch and knew their time on earth was almost done. When the sun rose, however, they saw that the battlefield was empty. The Navajos had no wish to face that deadly Hawken rifle again, so they fled in the night.

Chaves and Contreras built a crude litter and carried the feverish Tomás Baca over their back trail toward the Rio Grande. Late in the day they were found by the soldiers from Fort Craig.

Baca, though losing his leg, survived the ordeal and lived long in Socorro County. Contreras, who ransomed his son a few months afterward, later served in the territorial legislature at Santa Fe.

Of the encounter at Monica Spring, Manuel Chaves always claimed that it was his greatest fight. Giving credit to his foes, he declared that the Navajos displayed lofty courage, and had his own men showed any less, none would have lived to bear the tale.

THE STRANGE J.C. BROCK

NEW MEXICO HAS LONG BEEN KNOWN as a refuge for eccentric individualists. The old Santa Fe and Taos art colonies were a haven for such types. But in fact, every corner of the state has seen its share of mavericks.

A good example comes from Grant County in the person of Julius Caesar Brock, who died on March 19, 1952. His early years were spent on the wild Southwestern frontier.

Caesar, as he was always called, never knew for certain the identity of his father. One story, probably untrue, claimed he was the son of John Wilkes Booth, murderer of President Lincoln.

In any event, when the boy was seven, his mother fled with him in the middle of the night from the East Texas plantation where she had been working.

They landed at Fort Selden in the upper end of New Mexico's Mesilla Valley. Caesar's mother married the post sutler, Jack Yamens, and the youngster spent the next few years washing dishes for the soldiers.

About 1880 Yamens moved his family to a ranch he staked out on the west slope of the Burro Mountains. The location was roughly mid way between Silver City and the Arizona line.

Caesar spent his teens there, overworked and receiving occasional beatings from his step-father. To escape, he spent much time roaming the mountains alone on horseback.

J.C. Brock in his later years

On March 27, 1883, a neighbor rode in to advise Yamens that Apaches under Chato had slain some Arizona miners and were moving in their direction. Since his horse was worn out, he asked that Caesar, now 19, be sent down the front of the Burros to warn other ranchers.

As a capable, self-taught frontiersman, the young man eagerly jumped at the mission. He set out and by nightfall reached Knight's Ranch with the news, the last stop on his route. The next morning he started his return home.

Around 10:00 a.m. Caesar's trail crossed the road that came from Silver City and continued southwest toward Lordsburg. On the flat outside Thompson Canyon was a large walnut tree. He saw a hawk in the branches and took a shot at it.

Riding on, Caesar began to see Indian sign and became nervous. So he moved over to follow a ridge on the right, believing it gave him more protection.

Then he bumped into two mounted Apaches. But they wore red scarves tied around the head. Government scouts did that to identify themselves and not be mistaken for hostiles.

The scarves proved to be a ruse, though. These were a pair of Chato's raiders and they opened fire. Brock shot back, wounded one, and as he reported, "Both Apaches ran like old billy hell down the mountain."

Really worried now, Caesar circled around on his back trail, to be sure he didn't meet any more of the Indians.

A few hours later, he came down on the flat at the walnut tree where earlier he had shot at the hawk. Only now he found an abandoned buckboard with the still-warm bodies of a man and a woman nearby.

He recognized the victims as Judge H.C. McComas and his wife of Silver City. On their way to Lordsburg, they had accidentally stumbled into the path of Chato.

It occurred to Caesar that his thoughtless shot in the morning might have alerted the Apaches that someone was in the area, and thus led indirectly to the deaths of the couple. In any case, he quickly returned to his home ranch to spread word of the tragedy.

In later years, after Yamens drank himself to death, Brock struck out on his own. He took up residence in a cave and made his living by hunting deer and antelope. The meat he sold to boarding houses and hotels in Silver City, Lordsburg, and the mining camp of Shakespeare.

In that period, he went clad in patched overalls and wore moccasins. His uncut, tangled hair reached below the shoulders. Local folk referred to him as "a mountain man."

At age 40 Caesar Brock left his cave, trimmed his hair, and got married. He started his own ranch just outside Thompson Canyon within sight of the old walnut tree where the McComases died. As long as he lived, people came to interview him about that tragic event.

A few years ago Janaloo Hill, who lives in the ghost town of Shakespeare and who knew Julius Caesar Brock, guided me to the ruins of his ranch house. She also pointed out "the massacre tree," which still stands.

"Mr. Brock," she said, "was not what you could call a regular fellow. To the end, his behavior was pretty quirky. But he was a fascinating link to the past!"

Abandoned ranch house of J.C. Brock

IV

THE SOLDIER'S VIEW

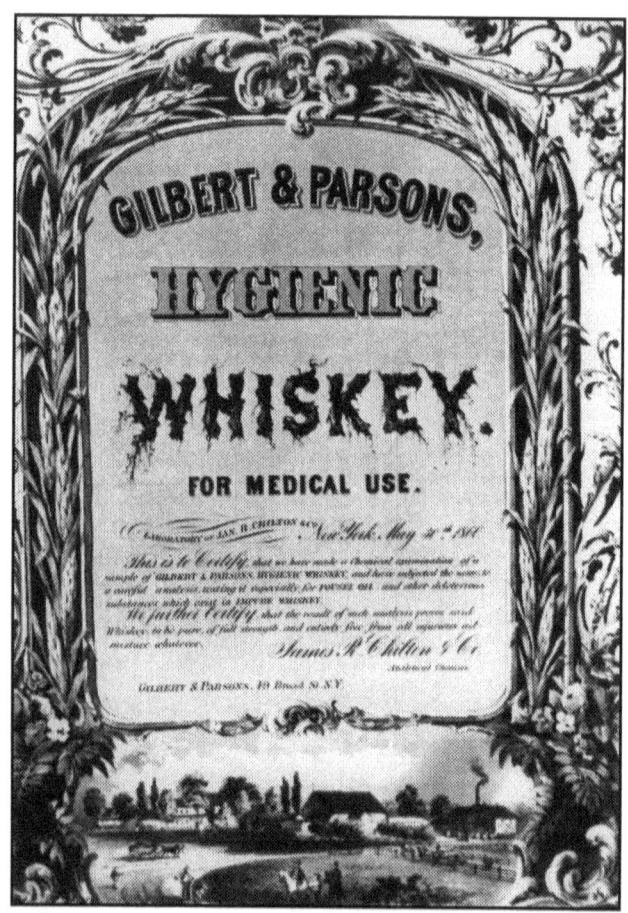

Hygienic Whiskey, a common item in fort hospitals on the New Mexico frontier. Used sometimes for other than medical purposes.

AN ARMY PROBLEM

AFTER STEPHEN W. KEARNY'S ARMY of the West seized New Mexico in 1846, the U.S. built a series of military posts to protect the territory. First came Fort Marcy, begun at Santa Fe that same year, then Fort Union was established east of Las Vegas in 1851.

In time, a string of garrisons extended from Fort Garland in the north, down the Rio Grande to huge Fort Craig below Socorro, and ending with Forts Selden and Fillmore in the Mesilla Valley. Later others were added on the east and west sides of the territory.

Duty at these isolated outposts was uncomfortable and dangerous. Not surprising, the dreary monotony took its toll in alcoholism.

Soldiers when drunk became unfit for duty, started brawls, and occasionally beat their wives, if they had one. The problem affected officers as much as enlisted men, harming discipline and health.

Most forts had a sutler's store operated by a civilian trader who was licensed and bonded by the government. He sold general merchandise and also liquor by the glass over his dry goods counter.

The trader was expected to follow rules, such as not selling spirits to a soldier already intoxicated. Post commanders had the authority to close down liquor sales if infractions persisted.

When that happened, troopers usually left the fort to get drunk at nearby "whiskey ranches" (also called "hog ranches"). Those were fly-by-night saloons just off the military reservation that sold rot gut whiskey at inflated prices.

Fort Marcy, located in the middle of Santa Fe, was different. Its soldiers when off duty could walk a couple of blocks to the plaza and find plenty of alcoholic drinks at competitive prices, as well as gambling going on night and day. That led Colonel Edwin V. Sumner in 1851 to refer to the capital as "a sink of vice."

A humorous incident occurred at Fort Wingate in 1863. General Kit Carson was temporary commander during the Navajo campaign.

Trying to curb drunkenness, he imposed a regulation that soldiers could not buy whiskey from the sutler without a permit signed by him.

An enlisted man who knew that the general couldn't read brought him a request for molasses. Kit promptly signed it, unaware that the document read whiskey rather than molasses. Word spread through the barracks and a flurry of "molasses" permits were applied for.

When General Carson learned that he had been conned, he was furious. Thereafter, he had his adjutant, Lieutenant Murphy, read aloud all his documents before signing them.

Initially, Indians and civilians were allowed to trade with the army sutler and also purchase liquor, by the glass, not the bottle. That was handy for them since no other store might exist within a hundred miles.

Under pressure from a growing temperance movement, the government in 1881 decided to halt all liquor sales at army posts. One sutler predicted, "The soldier will have his liquor, and will desert to get it."

In New Mexico, as elsewhere in the West, however, many troopers were accepting membership in the Good Templers, an international fraternal group dedicated to temperance.

Every man who joined was required to take a pledge that he would abstain from alcoholic drink. If he violated his pledge and nipped at the bottle, he might be expelled from the lodge. Occasionally, backsliders who repented were allowed to return.

Some years ago, while visiting Fort Union National Monument, Superintendent Homer Hastings showed me the location of the original Good Templers Lodge Hall, of which no trace remains today.

"It served as a kind of soldiers' clubhouse," he told me, "for non-alcoholic activities, of course." The walls were made of upright logs and the roof of rough timbers and earth. For that reason, no ruins survived.

I suggested that some kind of marker be placed at the site for the benefit of visitors. For after all, the Good Templers must have played an important role in the social life of the garrison.

The last time I checked, Washington had still not come through with funds for a marker.

Old Albuquerque, as Kit Carson saw it (After W.W.H. Davis)

MAJOR WYNKOOP RECALLS

IN EARLY 1862, Edward W. Wynkoop was an officer in the First Colorado Volunteers, a unit that marched south to help repel a Confederate invasion of New Mexico. He participated in the Battle of Valverde, February 21, which took place on the Rio Grande below Socorro.

There, Wynkoop first met Colonel Kit Carson who commanded a regiment of New Mexico volunteers. The two struck up a friendship that was to last until Carson's death six years later.

The following May, Carson and Wynkoop rode upriver to Albuquerque where Kit was to assume command of a garrison. As Major Wynkoop told it later, they traveled on the west side of the Rio Grande until they came to a ford opposite the city.

"The river was swollen from snows having recently melted in the mountains. As we prepared to swim our horses, we observed nearby two boats rapidly filling with gaily dressed señoritas on their way to church in Albuquerque, it being Sunday."

"Just as one of the boats pushed out with its fair freight," he continued, "a rough looking ranchero leaped from the bank into the boat. The navigator instantly backed his oars and ordered the man out, as his added weight endangered the lives of the ladies. The ranchero refused."

According to the Major, Kit Carson now intervened. In a mild voice, he explained the danger to the man and urged him to vacate the boat. When his words had no effect, he spoke in stronger tones.

But still the offender refused to budge. Then, in a flash Kit raised his sheathed sabre and struck him a tremendous blow alongside the head. The man was knocked backwards into the turbid waters of the Rio Grande and sank like lead.

"Quicker than thought," said Wynkoop, "Kit plunged in headfirst and dragged the fellow to the bank, thereby saving his life."

Over the next several months, Colonel Carson remained in charge of the Albuquerque troops. He knew little of formal military procedures, so he depended heavily upon a young lieutenant he called Mac, who had some regular army experience.

One day, as Wynkoop tells it, a native New Mexican soldier stole a horse and pistols and deserted. Shortly, he was captured, brought back, and lodged in the guardhouse.

After several weeks, Carson called Mac into his office and explained that the soldier in the guardhouse was eating up government rations. "I think it's time we punish him, but what's proper in these cases?"

The lieutenant replied that a court martial was in order and the penalty for desertion under military law was death by firing squad.

Recoiling in dismay, Kit answered, "Oh, we shouldn't go that far, Mac. Forget the court martial. Just call out the regimental band and drum the fellow out of the service and out of town."

So, Mac, being fond of military display, made the appropriate arrangements. Next day he assembled the band and sent a guard with fixed bayonets to drag the prisoner from his cell.

As the musicians struck up the Rogues March, a tune used on such occasions throughout the Civil War, the procession headed into the plaza. It took eight turns around the square, with the prisoner stepping lively to avoid the shining bayonets at his rear.

Albuquerque citizens had turned out in force. By the hundreds they lined the streets to view this most unusual spectacle.

From the plaza, the procession began to march up one avenue and down the other. The music, the drumming, and the tramping went on for several hours.

Finally, the lieutenant directed his parade toward Colonel Carson's headquarters. At the sound of its approach, Kit walked out on the porch to witness the conclusion of the proceedings. As he did so, he was heard to remark, "Now that Mac knows how to do things up right."

As the procession drew close, however, Kit stared and his jaw dropped. With frantic gestures, he summoned his lieutenant.

In a horrified voice, he announced, "Why Mac, that ain't the deserter. You got the wrong man!"

And, it was true. The guards had mistakenly taken another man who had been jailed overnight for drunkenness.

Major Wynkoop ended the tale by remarking, "I suppose the poor fellow thought that military law was rather strict when it came to having one too many drinks."

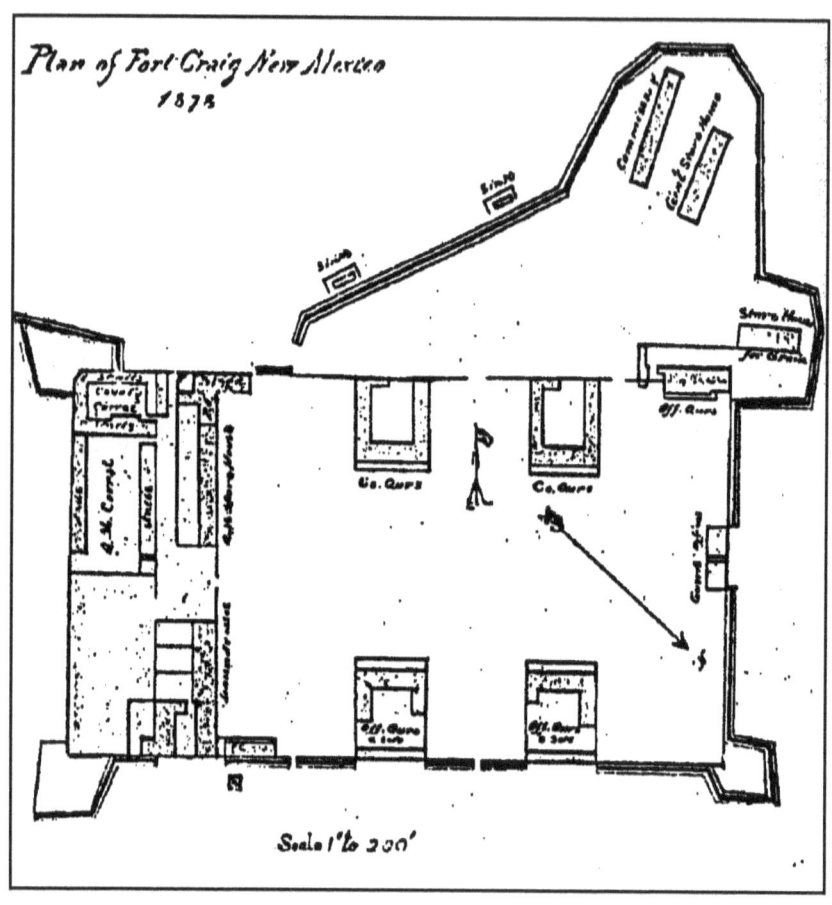

Plan of Fort Craig (National Archives)

SOLDIERING IN SOUTHERN NEW MEXICO

IN LATE SPRING, 1871, blond and slender Frederick Phelps graduated from West Point, promptly married his Ohio sweetheart, and shortly afterward applied for his first military assignment. As a West Point graduate and newly-commissioned second lieutenant, he was entitled to ask for a station anywhere he pleased.

"I'd read a book about New Mexico," he wrote later in his memoirs, "so, I requested to go there." For the green eastern lad, the rigors of the Territory proved unsettling, and not quite what his limited reading had led him to expect. Assigned to Fort Craig, located on the El Paso road south of Socorro, he described it as "one of the most desolate posts on the frontier."

Phelps' company commander was away upon his arrival, so he was ordered to take charge of the troop. It was a large responsibility for a youth just out of the academy. His first worry was that he wouldn't be able to handle all the paperwork. But the company sergeant soon showed him the bureaucratic ropes and that problem dissolved.

A more pressing question proved to be, could fuzz-faced Phelps win the respect of his duty-seasoned men? A few mornings after taking command, he got a chance to show what he was made of.

Time had come for the company to practice mounted drills. Lieutenant Phelps ordered the sergeant to bring a good horse to his quarters from the troop stables. When the animal was delivered, he found it to be "wall-eyed," that is, much of the eyeball was white. "I knew from my experience at West Point," he said afterward, "that a white-eyed horse generally had a bad temper. He cast one eye back toward me, and I knew at once that if I mounted in the usual manner by placing the left foot in the stirrup, he would throw me off before I could get fairly seated in the saddle."

To avoid that embarrassing outcome, he vaulted into the saddle in a single motion and had his boots firmly planted in the stirrups before the horse knew what had happened. But then the bucking began. Arching straight up, the animal came down stiff-legged on all fours, delivering a bone jarring blow to the rider.

Upon finding that he could not unseat the plucky lieutenant, the horse then bolted for the open plain where the troop was waiting to commence its drill. Reaching his men, Phelps yanked back on the heavy bit and his mount skidded to an abrupt stop. It was evident no one had expected him to stay on board and every soldier had a big grin on his face.

"I saw at once that some kind of a job had been put up on me," he continued. "If ever a troop got a good grinding drill, mine did that day. It was very hot and for two hours I never gave them a moment's rest. By the time the drill was over, they were heartily sick of it and anxious to get back."

Questioning his sergeant later, Phelps learned that no man had ever ridden the wall-eyed beast before. His performance had banished any notion that he was a soft kid-lieutenant. For the next six years, during his tour of duty in the Southwest, he kept that same horse, declaring that he "never rode a better one."

After only a few months at Fort Craig, Lieutenant Phelps was reassigned to another post. His journal notes, "From 1871 to 1876, I was stationed at Fort Bayard, a lonely, isolated place in southwest New Mexico, 100 miles west of La Mesilla. It was nestled at the upper end of a beautiful valley, on the north protected from the winter blasts by peaks of the Sierra Diablo and on the east by the crags of the Santa Rita, in which lie the famous Spanish copper mines."

While the natural setting was pleasing to the eye, the same could not be said for the fort itself. Phelps found that officers' quarters were mere huts made of logs and round stones. The flat dirt roofs leaked when it rained and "brought down rivulets of mud." The rough ceilings were home for tarantulas and centipedes. Being 600 miles from the railroad, the soldiers neither expected, nor got, much in the way of luxuries. The monotonous diet of government rations consisted of beef, bacon, coffee, sugar, and rice.

While at Bayard, much of Lieutenant Phelps' time was spent scouting for Indians who had jumped the reservation. In his first skirmish with Apaches, he confessed, "I was mightily scared, and only hoped I did not show it. But pride came to the rescue. I had once heard an experienced Indian fighter state that 'a man who says he is not afraid of Indians either don't know anything about it or he is a liar.'" In the ensuing attack upon a renegade village, the lieutenant admirably held up his end of the fight.

Over the next five years, Phelps became acquainted with much of the Territory. His campaigning and escort duty carried him from Fort Union on the plains to Fort Cummings in the desert north of Deming. When in 1876 he was transferred to a new station in south Texas, he looked back on his brief career in New Mexico and concluded that the worst and wildest outpost in the whole country had to be Fort Bayard. "The final jumping off place, sure enough," was the way he put it.

Parade Ground, Fort Stanton, New Mexico (National Archives photograph)

THE DEATH OF CAPTAIN STANTON

SEVERAL OF NEW MEXICO'S HISTORIC OLD FORTS were named for soldiers who gallantly gave their lives in battle, in the line of duty. Among them were Fort Wingate (for Captain Benjamin Wingate) east of Gallup, Fort Bascom (for Captain George Bascom) above Tucumcari, and Fort Bayard (for General George Bayard) outside Silver City.

And then there was Fort Stanton, located west of today's town of Lincoln. Its name honored Captain Henry W. Stanton, who was killed in the vicinity during January 1855 after a skirmish with Mescalero Apaches.

His slaying was part of a small but dramatic episode in the history of the Southwest's Indian wars. In fact, the incident is almost forgotten today.

Toward the end of 1854, the Mescaleros staged a series of raids up the Pecos Valley, and then fled with stolen livestock to their winter camps in the high country below Sierra Blanca Peak.

Troops stationed on the Rio Grande were ordered out, right after New Year's, on a campaign to find and punish the hostiles. The weather was cold and snowy, not a pleasant prospect for the soldiers.

The first to march were 81 men of the First Dragoons from Fort Thorn (near Hatch). Their commander was Captain Richard S. Ewell, a tough bald-headed officer who would win fame a few years later in the Civil War as one of Robert E. Lee's best generals.

From Fort Fillmore, below Mesilla, another force set out under Captain Henry Stanton, a man described by his fellow soldiers as "a perfect officer and gentleman." Stanton kissed his wife goodbye and told her to expect him back within two weeks.

The two units came together at a rendezvous in the foothills of the Sacramento Mountains and then began climbing through heavy forest. Mescalero scouts were watching their every move, and soon began to oppose the advance with sniper attacks and by setting fire to the dry grass.

In his official report, Captain Ewell wrote, "The Indians seemed in force with every mark of defiance and during the whole day they obstructed our march, disputing every ravine with arrow shots."

In this series of running attacks, the Captain guessed about fifteen Mescaleros were shot from their horses, noting that "their bodies were quickly carried off by comrades, leaving the ground marked with blood." The Apaches claimed later that they had lost twelve men, including a chief.

Late in the afternoon, the troopers came upon the main tepee village, now abandoned. Ewell occupied it and prepared to spend the night. Suddenly, another village was discovered a short distance away, and Stanton cut out a few of his men and went to investigate.

It too stood empty and the Captain followed a broad trail of its fleeing occupants that led toward the timber. In so doing, he and his party fell into an ambush.

As the soldiers retreated toward their camp under heavy fire, Stanton bravely placed himself between the enemy and his men and blazed away with his Sharps carbine. But a shot from the Mescaleros struck him square in the forehead and he was killed instantly.

Two additional soldiers died before a relief party arrived from Ewell and dispersed the attackers. Bodies of the fallen were recovered and carried to camp for burial.

After a quick funeral next day, Captain Ewell guided the entire troop south in search of the Apaches. But by reading smoke signals, he shortly learned that they were in full flight toward the Guadalupe Mountains, so he gave up the chase.

As the troop returned and passed by the fresh graves of Captain Stanton and his men, they were horrified to find that wolves had dug up and half-eaten the corpses and ravens had picked out their eyes.

A bonfire was hastily built, the remains burned, and the charred bones were collected and taken back to Fort Thorn. From there, a special detail was sent to Fort Fillmore, carrying the small box that contained what was left of Captain Stanton.

Private James Bennett, who was along, wrote in his diary, "We rode into the fort. Mrs. Stanton stood in the door awaiting her husband. Poor woman! She asks for him. The answer is evaded. Her smiles are fled and tears stain her cheek. Him she loved, she never more shall behold."

A few months later, Captain Stanton's gold watch, taken from his pocket at the time of his death, was recovered from the Mescaleros. The governor of New Mexico saw that it was returned to his widow.

In May of 1855 the army built a new fort to control the Mescaleros and decided that it should bear the lamented Captain's name. Fort Stanton had a long and turbulent history, until it was abandoned as a military post in 1896.

Engraving: Marcy's Winter Expedition (After Captain Randolph Marcy)

WHEN "MARY ANN" SAVED THE DAY

IN THE HEYDAY of the Rocky Mountain fur trade, one seldom found Hispanic New Mexicans trapping beaver. An exception was Mariano Medina, a companion of such famous mountain men as Kit Carson and Jim Bridger.

Born at Taos about 1812, Mariano was said to have some Indian and French blood. His early history is obscure, but by the time he comes to view in the 1840s he is already an accomplished trapper.

In that decade, the price of beaver collapsed in eastern markets. Like others in the trade, Mariano Medina sought another way to make a living. For a time he guided emigrants over the Oregon Trail, then operated a ferry at a river crossing on the same route.

By 1858 Medina was scouting for the U.S. Army during the so-called Utah War. Persecuted Mormons had fled to that distant territory, from which calls for independence soon echoed.

President James Buchanan in Washington thought the matter was serious enough to dispatch a 2,500-man army to Utah to maintain order.

When a Mormon elder in Salt Lake City heard that, he belittled the threat in a speech, saying: "Good God! I have wives enough to wipe out that army."

Receiving news of this statement, the *Santa Fe Gazette* editorialized: "If they fight as well as they boast, our soldiers will have some trouble."

Colonel Albert Sidney Johnston and his force reached Utah and set up winter camp. But supplies ran short, so the colonel decided to send a junior officer, Captain Randolph B. Marcy, to Taos, the nearest place that food and equipment could be purchased.

Marcy set out in the dead of winter with 26 civilian packers and 40 soldiers. One of his guides was Mariano Medina.

It seems that troops from the East, knowing no Spanish, heard his first name as "Mariana," and then translated it as Mary Ann.

Captain Marcy and his relief expedition crossed several mountain ranges and climbed over Cochetope Pass in western Colorado. Then their luck deserted them.

A furious storm left deep snow and hid the trail. Rations gave out, and most of the pack animals died from the cold or were run off by Indians. Soon the exhausted men faced starvation.

Captain Marcy asked Mary Ann whether he could reach Fort Massachusetts in the San Luis Valley above Taos and bring back aid. Medina said yes and promised to return within six or seven days.

That interval passed, but there was no sign of their messenger or help. By the eleventh day, all agreed in despair that Medina had perished in the cold. Yet, a few hours later he dashed up on a fresh horse with word that army wagons with food and medicine were only ten miles behind him.

In his memoirs, Marcy wrote: "Some of my men laughed, danced, and screamed with delight while others cried like children." And he added, "I offered up sincere thanks to the Almighty for delivering us from a horrible death by starvation."

Mary Ann, of course, was the hero of the moment. Knowing that the men were craving tobacco as much as food, he had brought a large plug of Cavendish that he cut into bits and distributed.

After a brief rest at Fort Massachusetts, Marcy's column continued on to Taos. The first thing the captain did upon arrival was pay Mary Ann a bonus of $500. At the time, this was a staggering amount.

Said Marcy, "I thought that would be sufficient to supply all his wants for a long period." Imagine the officer's shock when the next morning Mary Ann approached him and asked for a loan of $5. He had lost all of his money the night before at cards.

Without a moment's hesitation, Marcy handed over the small sum requested, with the mild suggestion that the guide should in the future avoid the gambling tables.

Mariano Medina in his last years settled with his Indian wife and children on the Big Thompson River near today's Loveland, Colorado. Here he died in 1878.

Medina had been a well-known figure in Denver, and the city's leading newspaper carried an impressive obituary. Among others, it quoted Randolph B. Marcy, now an Army general.

Remembering his former guide's heroics, Marcy declared that on the 1858 march to Taos, Medina had saved his expedition from total annihilation. Mary Ann would have been pleased that by such words his service was remembered and honored.

Kit Carson (After D. Peters)

AN ARTIST IN SANTA FE, 1865

ARTIST WORTHINGTON WHITTREDGE, of a prominent eastern family, visited New Mexico's capital for several months in 1865. He traveled with General John Pope who was conducting an inspection of forts in the Territory.

Whittredge was a member of the so-called Hudson River School of artists. Heavily influenced by European romanticism, these painters chose spectacular landscapes as their main subject.

As one spokesman for the group commented, "This led to much wandering of our artists."

While attached to the General's staff, Whittredge, got the opportunity to capture on canvas breath-taking scenes of desert, mesas, and mountains.

From his autobiography come a couple of amusing anecdotes about incidents occurring in Santa Fe during his stay.

The painter was given quarters in the barracks of old Fort Marcy. Great was his elation when he discovered the identity of his roommate. It was none other than the legendary Kit Carson.

An officer in the New Mexico Volunteers, Kit had been summoned to give General Pope a report on the state of Indian hostilities.

Of his companion, Whittredge remarked, "He never turned in without first examining his revolver and placing it under his pillow, and he awakened at the slightest noise." From a lifetime on the frontier, Kit had become cautious.

Inasmuch as a celebrated general and his staff were in town, a fancy ball was arranged in their honor. Santa Fe society was all atitter, both men and women dashing about to prepare proper dress.

Poor Kit Carson was the most perplexed man in town. Knowing little about social graces, he had heard rumors that pumps were required on formal occasions. But he had no idea what they were.

"He hated to ask any of the officers how to dress, so he finally asked me," Whittredge said. "I told him pumps were a sort of low shoe but that no army officer would think of wearing pumps at a ball, and that he must go in his boots."

But that was not enough for Kit. Still uncertain, he hurried around to Santa Fe shops to see what he could find.

One merchant finally produced a pair of lady's slippers that supposedly resembled pumps. They were tried on, fitted Carson perfectly, and he paid a high price for them.

That evening at the door of the ballroom, he took his artist friend aside and explained that he had the pumps hidden on his person.

Once inside, if he found the officers did not use them, then he would keep his boots on. But if necessary, he had the expensive pumps ready to wear.

The men, in fact, were all wearing boots, as Whittredge quickly observed. But for a moment, he writes, "it was difficult for me to see where Colonel Carson in his tight-fitting uniform had managed to hide his slippers."

"On closer inspection, it was evident that he had buttoned one on each side of his breast until his figure was not unlike that of the handsome *señoras* whirling in the waltz."

While at Santa Fe, the artist climbed Cerro Gordo to make a sketch. A rough-looking frontiersman, with a broken nose and hair matted like a buffalo, rode by and paused to watch the progress at the easel.

Finally he announced that he was going to "buy that picture." When Whittredge replied that it wasn't for sale, the man waved a huge pistol and repeated his demand.

With a steady eye, the painter declared, "My friend, I'm from New York and I sell my pictures for a thundering price. You can have this one for $10,000 and if you want a frame that will be $2,000 more!"

In Whittredge's words, "That silenced him. He put up his pistol, marched off, and I have never seen him since."

A mini-biography of Worthington Whittredge can be found in most standard references on 19th century American art.

Hopi Snake Dancer (After John G. Bourke)

CAPTAIN BOURKE
AND THE SNAKE DANCES

CAPTAIN JOHN G. BOURKE was one of the scholarly U.S. Army officers of the latter 1800s who spent his leisure hours in the field recording the customs and lore of western Indians. His several published books and articles on that subject remain of value today.

In 1881 he received a year's leave from the Army to carry out his observations and research in the Southwest. The captain selected Santa Fe as his headquarters, calling it, "a quaint and ever-curious town."

On August 3, Bourke departed the capital in a military ambulance, at that time used also for general transportation. He headed downriver for Santo Domingo Pueblo where he attended the August 4 corn dance, to this day a major event drawing large numbers of visitors.

But the Army officer had his eyes focused on something more spectacular than a mere corn dance. His ultimate destination on this trip was the Hopi villages on isolated mesas in northeastern Arizona. He meant to watch and take notes on the late summer snake dances of the Hopi Indians.

From what Bourke had heard, the ritual, openly performed, was an extraordinary marvel. The Antelope Priests danced with live rattlesnakes in their mouths, and after the ceremony was completed they released the snakes in the desert to carry messages to the gods asking for rain.

When Spaniards explored the upper Rio Grande in the 16th century, they found that many Indians of the area had rituals involving the use of snakes. The performances were held in the village plazas and seeing them for the first time, Christian soldiers were both awed and disgusted. One of them, remarking upon a particularly large rattler, wrote, "We thought this snake might be the devil, who has them enslaved."

One of the earliest accounts comes from the pen of Hernán Gallegos with the Chamuscado expedition that entered New Mexico in 1581. That party witnessed a snake dance in a Piro pueblo of the Socorro Valley.

"Two Indians carrying rattlesnakes in their hands walk around in the midst of the people," said Gallegos. "The snakes are real; you can hear their rattles. They coil around the necks and creep all over the bodies of the two Indians who come dancing."

"Then the pair give the snakes to their leader who lets them crawl up his body, making a great deal of noise with their rattles, until they reach his throat. He swings around quickly and the snakes fall to the ground. Other Indians put the reptiles in their mouths and leave."

For Europeans, the snake was a symbol of evil. So not surprisingly in later years Spanish padres and civil authorities worked hard to suppress the Pueblo dances. They met with considerable success, except among the isolated Hopis in Arizona.

On his western journey, Captain Bourke stopped at Zuni and interviewed the Indian governor of the pueblo. He was told that "in the good old times, all the Pueblos had the rattlesnake-dance. But we Zunis gave it up because of outside pressure."

Upon reaching the Hopi, Bourke ascended First Mesa and received a warm welcome, even when he intruded into a sacred kiva.

Evidently, he was accorded other privileges because the Indians had gotten the idea that he was a representative of the President in Washington. What they failed to understand was that the captain would be writing a book, disclosing the details of their snake rituals.

With his keen eye, Bourke noted all the fine points of the lengthy dance. For example, he wrote: "After the snakes had been carried in the mouths of dancers, they were dropped on the ground, sprinkled with sacred cornmeal, picked up by small boys and passed to the chief priest who prayed over them."

When in 1884, John G. Bourke published what he had seen and experienced in a 370 page book, readers in the East were both shocked and fascinated. One outcome of that was that the number of curious visitors clamoring to see the snake dances soared.

By the end of the century, the Indians were complaining that the multitudes of tourists were overwhelming them. Nevertheless, access to the dances remained fairly open until the 1960s, when the hippie invasion and fleets of chartered buses bringing seniors from California brought an end to the liberal admittance policies of the past.

V

MEN OF STANDING

Judge Spruce Baird (After C. Wharton)

A TEXAN JUDGE IN NEW MEXICO

DURING THE DECADE OF THE 1840s, Texans were not held in high esteem in New Mexico. The Texas-Santa Fe Expedition, sent from Austin in 1841 to open trade, was captured by Governor Manuel Armijo and its members sent to a lock-up in Mexico. In retaliation, Texans raided New Mexican caravans moving east over the Santa Fe Trail. Mothers in those years threatened their children by telling them, "If you're not good I'll let the *Tejanos* come and get you."

After Texas was admitted to the Union as a state, late in 1845, it asserted an old claim to all of New Mexico east of the Rio Grande. That attempted land-grab did not increase the Texans' popularity.

Out of the disputed area, the Texas legislature created, on paper, Santa Fe County and a new judicial district. The governor appointed Spruce McCoy Baird, a Nacogdoches lawyer, as judge of the district and gave him instructions to go to Santa Fe. There he was to organize the county under the laws of Texas and represent the interests of the state in the hullabaloo that was sure to follow.

Thirty-four year old Baird climbed on a stagecoach and headed west, prepared to do his best in tackling an impossible job. In Santa Fe political leaders rebuffed him and the people ignored him. The local press, intimating that the judge from Texas was a public nuisance, suggested a tar and feathering.

For two years, Judge Baird rambled up and down the Rio Grande as far as El Paso, serving as a spokesman for the Texas claim, but achieving no tangible results. Then in 1850 the U.S. Congress settled the matter. It established the present boundary between the two states and provided Texas 10 million dollars for giving up its claim to eastern New Mexico. Spruce Baird was out of a job.

During his stay, he had grown to love the land and people, so instead of returning to Nacogdoches, he decided to settle down in New Mexico. In the valley south of Albuquerque, he purchased a thirty-three thousand acre ranch and not far from the east bank of the Rio Grande began building a home. It was constructed, not of adobe bricks, but of *terrones*, which were sod blocks cut from the river bottoms. As soon as the dirt mansion was completed he brought his wife out from Texas.

The Bairds raised four children in their house by the Rio Grande. And over the years they entertained many travelers. The old Camino Real, the main Albuquerque to El Paso road, passed just a hundred feet from their front door. Territorial attorney William W.H. Davis was one of those who found overnight lodging at the Baird Ranch. In later years he wrote in his memoirs that he had been "treated with genuine southern hospitality, and had passed a pleasant evening with his host and hostess."

In spite of his Texan origin, Spruce Baird got along well in New Mexico. He was admitted to the bar and took part in many famous trials of the period. In 1852 and 1853 he served as a special agent to the Navajos. He was appointed territorial attorney general in 1860, but resigned after six months because Indians were raiding in the vicinity of Albuquerque and he wanted to go home from Santa Fe and protect his family.

Baird was known among local people as *El Chino Tejano*, The Curly-Haired Texan, because of his mop of red, curly hair. He was courteous and fair to all, and of the native New Mexicans he once declared that he "had never had better neighbors in any country." And on another occasion, he added that they were "the most orderly people he had ever seen."

Spruce Baird's fortunes crashed in 1862. When General H.H. Sibley's Confederate army marched up from El Paso and took Albuquerque, he threw in his lot with the South. But after Sibley was forced to retreat a few months later, Baird found it necessary to uproot his family, abandon the ranch, and flee. For his "treason," the Federal government confiscated his property.

Making his way to San Antonio, he deposited his wife and children there, while he went off to serve as a Confederate officer in eastern Texas and Louisiana. By the end of the war he was penniless.

Realizing that there was no future for him in Texas, and with his Albuquerque ranch gone, Baird went to Trinidad, Colorado and opened a law office in 1867. He was down in Cimarron, New Mexico hearing a case in 1872 when he died suddenly.

One day I went looking for the ruins of Spruce Baird's old ranch house below Albuquerque. Following directions given me by journalist Howard Bryan, I finally located the place off south Second Street—grown up in weeds and surrounded by a cornfield. Twenty years ago lightning had destroyed one wing of the house, and a later fire had charred the old roof beams and ceiling. But for all that abuse and neglect, the rambling building still stood, its walls in places more than two feet thick.

As I wandered through the desolate and empty rooms, there was nothing but silence. Yet it was not hard to imagine the house in a happier day when children had played there, guests had found hospitality, and the Chino Tejano had ruled his beautiful and productive estate. Several years after my visit, a new owner of the property bulldozed the ruins, probably having no idea of their historical significance.

Portion of the Baird House, below Albuquerque

Bishop (later Archbishop) John B. Lamy
(Museum of New Mexico photograph)

HANG THE BISHOP!

IN THE SUMMER OF 1851 occurred an unseemly episode in the capital city of the Territory of New Mexico. Main figures in the little drama were Bishop John B. Lamy and Chief Justice Grafton Baker.

Judge Baker had been appointed to his office by President Millard Fillmore and traveled to New Mexico in the company of Colonel Edwin V. Sumner, the new military commander of the Southwest.

A man said to be "splendidly trained in the law," Baker was also pompous and arrogant. A Southerner by upbringing, he had no knowledge of customs and conditions in the strange land of New Mexico.

John B. Lamy was equally conscious of his status and authority. French-born, he had accepted the office of bishop with some misgivings, because his new diocese was so huge. It included such distant cities as El Paso and Tucson.

The bishop and the chief justice arrived at Santa Fe within weeks of one another and took up their offices. In a matter of days, a serious dispute developed.

At the center of contention was the old Spanish military chapel, known as the Castrense, located on the plaza opposite the Governor's Palace. In colonial days, it had served the soldiers of the royal garrison.

Upon seizing Santa Fe in 1846, at the outbreak of the Mexican War, American troops found the Castrense boarded up and its roof nearing collapse. Still in place was a beautiful stone altar screen, carved in the previous century.

The new civil authorities took possession of the dilapidated chapel and used it for storage or other purposes. Initially, no one in Santa Fe seemed to object.

Upon his arrival, Chief Justice Baker decided it was a perfect place to hold the first session of the district court. He had the floor swept and cobwebs cleared and in front of the altar installed his bench.

While this was going on, the judge was also making enemies. He had come from his native Mississippi with a black slave, something the people of Santa Fe held against him.

But beyond that Baker made no secret of his disdain for the capital's residents. Editor William Kephart of the "Santa Fe Weekly Gazette" charged that His Honor was "going about the streets trying to pick quarrels and get up fights with our citizens."

Kephart, who was also a Protestant missionary on the side, further condemned the judge for his excessive drinking. It was strong drink, probably El Paso brandy, that led to trouble.

Judge Baker convened court and began to impanel a jury. Among those summoned was former governor Donaciano Vigil who refused jury duty. He said some of his ancestors were buried under the floor of the Castrense and it was not fitting in any case to hold court in a chapel.

Bishop Lamy was in full agreement and in fact had already requested the civil government to return custody of the Castrense to the Catholic Church. Judge Baker had refused.

The same evening, following Vigil's protest, Judge Baker took to drinking in one of the plaza saloons. In slurred speech, he was heard to say loudly that, if they continued to oppose him, he would see Bishop Lamy and his assistant, Father Joseph Machebeuf, hang from the same gallows!

Next morning his remarks spread throughout the city, causing outrage. Indeed, an angry mob collected in front of the judge's house, howling for his head.

In terror, the chief justice rushed a message to Colonel Sumner pleading for protection. The colonel refused to provide it.

In the nick of time, Father Machebeuf, sent by the bishop, came hurrying up and placed himself between the mob and the hapless judge.

Having his life saved in this manner, Judge Baker was understandably contrite. Marching straight to the bishop's residence, he apologized profusely for his indiscretion.

On the following day, in open court he turned the Castrense over to Bishop Lamy in the presence of the territorial governor and other officials. One room in the old adobe palace was afterward set aside for the use of the court.

Foes tried unsuccessfully to have Baker removed from office. But upon conclusion of his term in 1853, the president declined to reappoint him to the bench.

Incidentally, a short time afterward, Bishop Lamy decided the Castrense was not worth saving and he ordered it demolished. But the stone altar screen was saved and can be seen today in Santa Fe's Cristo Rey Church.

Amado Chaves, assisted Ambrosio Abeytia in Washington D.C.

GOVERNOR ABEYTIA'S DEBT

MANY YEARS AGO MY GOOD FRIEND Consuelo Chaves Summers of Santa Fe asked my help in organizing her father's papers. Amado Chaves had been raised on the New Mexico frontier, served as the Territory's first Superintendent of Public Education, and had been elected Santa Fe's mayor. He died in 1930.

Among Amado's papers was a brief personal history that gave details of his early life. I made a copy of that document before we delivered the entire collection to the State Archives.

I ran upon the item in my files the other day and discovered it contained a fascinating story about Ambrosio Abeytia, once the Indian governor of Isleta Pueblo. That village was the parent community of Ysleta del Sur, founded downriver in the El Paso Valley at the time of the 1680 Pueblo Revolt.

Toward the close of the Civil War, Abeytia was invited to attend a meeting at the hacienda of New Mexico Governor Henry Connelly, located at Peralta a few miles from Isleta. Amado Chaves says that Abeytia was an able man, fluent in Spanish, and quite rich.

At the meeting, the army paymaster told Governor Connelly that they faced a crisis because the soldiers had not been paid for many months, owing to the difficulties of communication with Washington. Thereupon, Connelly asked Ambrosio Abeytia for a patriotic loan, to bail out the territorial government.

Abeytia readily agreed and asked them to wait while he rode home to get the money. He soon returned and handed over $18,000 in American gold coins. The paymaster gave him a receipt and said the treasury would make good on the loan in due course.

Some months later the Civil War ended. Time drifted by, General Ulysses S. Grant was elected president in 1868 and four years later he won reelection for a second term. Still, Ambrosio Abeytia waited patiently for the government to give him his money back.

Now in his eighties he began to fear he would die without ever getting it. So, he decided to go to Washington to see what could be done. As companions on the long trip, he enlisted Isleta's lieutenant governor as well as the U.S. Indian agent for the Territory.

Amado Chaves declared that the agent was a very capable and polished gentleman, but added that "he was overly fond of liquor and would remain in a state of intoxication for weeks."

"In 1866 I was sent by my father to school in Washington, D.C., arriving not knowing a word of English. Upon graduation, I was appointed a clerk in the Pension Bureau of the Interior Department," Chaves adds.

One morning he read in the newspaper that a delegation from New Mexico, headed by Ambrosio Abeytia, had arrived in the capital and was lodged at the Metropolitan Hotel. Knowing all three men named in the paper, he went immediately to offer them his services.

Chaves found the two Isletans in great distress. Unable to speak a word of English, they were completely dependent upon the Indian agent, who had remained in a drunken state since their arrival. They'd not even been able to order a meal.

Taking charge, the young Chaves admonished the agent to sober up, so he could go with the Indians to visit the President. Then, he sent for some food and afterwards took the Isletans sightseeing and to the theater.

"As the agent continued drunk for three days," writes Chaves, "I finally conducted the Indians myself to see President Grant. I acted as interpreter for them."

"The President greeted us cordially. The Indians were delighted to meet the Great White Father. Governor Abeytia presented his old paymaster's receipt and humbly asked if he could have his money back."

Grant was astonished over the long delay and wanted to know why Abeytia had waited so long to request payment. The governor replied that he had been ashamed to ask the Great White Father for his money. It seemed undignified.

Toward the end of the interview, President Grant suddenly asked his visitors whether they had been enjoying their stay in Washington. To their astonishment, he posed the question in perfect Spanish.

At once they wanted to know where he had learned the language. He had gotten some Spanish at West Point, the President said, and had learned more during his service in the Mexican War and afterward while stationed at New Mexico's Fort Fillmore in the Mesilla Valley.

"All the young officers at Fillmore," Grant explained, "used to go to nearby Las Cruces to attend dances. I had a very dear young lady friend there, the beautiful Señorita Marguerita Ascarate, daughter of a prominent family."

As it turned out, President Grant had to arrange for Amado Chaves to escort the Isleta Indians home, since the agent was too drunk to do it.

Shortly after his return, Ambrosio Abeytia received his $18,000 from the U.S. government, plus a substantial sum in interest. He was delighted, not only to get the money but also because his faith in the Great White Father had been vindicated.

Kit Carson's Home, Taos

SENATOR DOOLITTLE TOURS NEW MEXICO

AT DAWN ON NOVEMBER 29, 1864, Colonel John M. Chivington led his 3rd Colorado Volunteers in an attack upon a Cheyenne village located on Sand Creek in southeastern Colorado. That bloody morning almost two hundred Indians died, mostly women and children.

The Cheyennes, flying an American flag, were actually under the protection of the U.S. Army. But Chivington and his local volunteers paid no attention to that. They were seeking revenge for earlier raids by the tribe on Colorado citizens.

The Sand Creek Massacre produced shock waves across the country. Dismayed by the event, Congress voted to send out west a commission of its own members to investigate and report back on the condition of the Indian tribes.

Republican Senator James R. Doolittle from Wisconsin was named head of this touring body. Another member was Connecticut Senator Lafayette Foster, who at the time was serving as president pro tem of the Senate.

The commission, with its escort and staff, departed from Fort Leavenworth, Kansas in May of 1865 for a trip over the Santa Fe Trail. We are unclear whether word of Lincoln's assassination, April 14, had reached the party before it left, or whether a messenger caught up with it on the prairie.

Since Vice President Andrew Johnson had assumed the Presidency, Senator Foster, being next in line (as the senate's president pro tem) in effect became Vice President. Since he remained on the tour, he would be the highest ranking government official thus far to visit the Southwest. His presence caused quite a stir.

Doolittle and his associates stopped first at Fort Lyon, Colorado, the closest place to the massacre site. They conducted interviews and gathered information before moving on to New Mexico.

At Fort Union east of Las Vegas, the senators left the Santa Fe Trail and turned south to Fort Sumner on the Pecos River. They wished to see how the Navajos, held there since their defeat the previous year, were faring. Then they traveled on to Santa Fe.

The Congressional delegation was surprised to find that a huge procession had come out from the capital to meet them at the Arroyo Hondo, a few miles east of the city. It was led by Governor Henry Connelly and Chief Justice Kirby Benedict.

The throng wended its way to the plaza for welcoming speeches in front of the Palace of the Governors. Afterward, according to the *Santa Fe Gazette*, Fort Marcy soldiers fired "a salute in honor of the Vice President of the United States." Foster was getting most of the attention.

Their last night in town, the senators were treated to a reception ball, or fandango, its strangeness causing them no little amazement. Then they left for Denver, by way of Taos.

At the latter place, the travelers, wrote Senator Doolittle, stayed overnight in the hospitable home of Kit Carson and his wife Josefa. Based on his long experience with them, Carson was considered an expert on Indians. He angrily referred to Chivington's attack as "that murderous massacre at Sand Creek."

That evening, after Kit had finished his testimony on Indian affairs, he seemed willing to relate an incident or two from his adventurous career. As Doolittle noted, Vice President Foster drew him out and he gave a remarkable account of his escape from the clutches of a great grizzly bear. The visitors listened raptly far into the night.

One wonders how the Carsons were able to accommodate the senators and their staffs in their modest and rather rustic adobe residence. The eastern gentlemen by this time must have grown used to primitive conditions in the West.

In Denver, the last stop on their fact-finding tour, the Congressmen held a public meeting in the large Opera House. Upon explaining that the Plains Indians would have to be placed on reservations and taught to farm, they were met with cries from the hostile crowd: "Exterminate them! Exterminate them!"

That outburst, and all else they had experienced on their odyssey, undoubtedly provided plenty of food for thought as they journeyed back to Washington.

Lucien Maxwell

STRANGE MR. MAXWELL

NEW MEXICO HISTORY IS LITTERED with stories of eccentric characters. It is no exaggeration to say that the Land of Enchantment has been a breeding ground for oddball men and women—people who lived according to their own lights and snubbed society's polite conventions.

Lucien Bonaparte Maxwell easily qualifies as a member of that select crowd. As a scout for the Fremont Expedition of 1842 and owner of the million acre Maxwell Land Grant, he carved his name in western history. But it was his curious ways of behavior that made him a legend in his own day.

Most tales of his eccentricities date from the period after 1857 when he was settled comfortably in an adobe mansion on the Little Cimarron River. The site was located forty miles below Raton Pass on the Santa Fe Trail.

The Maxwell residence, center of the sprawling land grant, contained two stories and abundant rooms. From the upper windows could be seen great herds of cattle and sheep grazing on the plains to the east. An early visitor remarked, "The surroundings and whole atmosphere of the place remind me of baronial estates in Europe of the Middle Ages."

Agents of the Barlow & Sanderson Stage Line persuaded "Old Maxwell," as he was then called, to accommodate their passengers at his house. That was not difficult, for the wealthy owner had a long-standing policy that any traveler calling at his door would be fed and sheltered at no cost. Such liberal hospitality was characteristic of the frontier.

Maxwell had two huge dining rooms, the second one for women who were segregated, in line with prevailing New Mexican custom. On occasion, up to twenty men might be seated around the table, all partaking of a free meal. The many bedrooms available to guests were carpeted but had no furniture. At night, servants appeared and unrolled mattresses on the floor for bedding.

One cold March evening, the coach arrived and among the passengers was a fancy-dressed, well educated man from New York. After a good night's sleep and hearty breakfast, he asked the stage driver to point out the landlord. The driver nodded toward Maxwell who was just heading out the door.

The New Yorker stepped up to his host and asked, "How much do I owe you for lodging and breakfast?"

"Nothing!" was the reply.

"But I am a stranger and do not wish to accept a favor," the man said. "I want to pay for what I have gotten."

An angry Maxwell snorted, "Well then, it is $20, damn it."

Astonished at the amount, the New Yorker stared at Maxwell for a moment and then handed him a $20 bill. His host took the money and without saying a word walked to the fireplace where he threw the bill into the flames. Lucien Maxwell would not be insulted under his own roof.

Although a rich man and a founder of the First National Bank of Santa Fe, Maxwell's utter disregard for money contributed to his reputation for peculiar conduct. A story he often told on himself further illustrates the point.

Once Maxwell went to nearby Fort Union to collect for a hay and corn contract he had completed. On arrival, the paymaster delivered to him $39,000 in cash. Maxwell stuffed the money into his saddle bags and started for home.

Back at Cimarron, he went into his stable, threw the saddle into the corner, and turned out his horse. Days later, needing a large sum of money to make a payment, he rummaged about in his room. But all his searching failed to turn up the Fort Union cash.

Calling his wife, Maxwell asked her where was that $39,000 he had brought from the fort. She disclaimed any knowledge of its whereabouts and then scolded him for being so careless.

A week later a stable boy brought to the house some torn pieces of greenbacks. It suddenly dawned on Maxwell that he had left his money in the saddlebags. Rushing out, he discovered that hogs had gotten in the bags and eaten part of the contents. The bulk of the bills, however, were recovered.

In 1868 Maxwell developed the Aztec gold mine in the mountains to the west. Over an eight month period, he made $100,000 on the venture. Leaving the mine and heading down the canyon toward his ranch, he was in the habit of tossing a sack of gold dust, worth several thousand dollars, into the back of his wagon.

More than once the sack bounced out and came to rest in the middle of the road. But every time it was found by a passing farmer or Indian, who knew unquestionably that Maxwell was the owner. And the gold was always returned.

In 1870 Lucien Maxwell sold his land grant to a group of capitalists for more than a million dollars. Much of that sum he lost through poor investments, so that he had to return to ranching at Fort Sumner on the Pecos River. There he died in 1875 and was buried in the local cemetery.

Close by his grave, six years later, another bizarre character in New Mexico history was buried—Billy the Kid.

Franz Huning, a German New Mexican

A GERMAN NEW MEXICAN

OF ALL THE PIONEER BUILDERS of nineteenth century New Mexico, Franz Huning has to be numbered among the most unusual and dynamic. A native of Hanover, Germany he left home in his teens intending to make his fortune in far off California.

Arriving in St. Louis early in 1849, Franz found the place full of German immigrants, like himself, and cholera claiming victims by the score. Luckily, he soon landed a job as a bullwhacker on a wagon train headed for New Mexico.

He was two months on the trail, reaching Santa Fe on Christmas Day. The color of the town and its inhabitants so enchanted him that he gave up all thought of California. His fortune, if he was to have one, would be found in New Mexico.

According to what his grandson wrote later, young Franz went completely native. Within a year he had learned to speak, read and write Spanish so that he often went months without using English. One of his textbooks was a battered copy of *Don Quixote*.

He took an assortment of odd jobs and then in 1851 he joined a party of twenty-seven New Mexicans who were going on a trading expedition among the Apaches of Arizona. Franz bought a small stock of trade goods, loaded them on a burro, and thereby became a merchant.

The men continued all the way down to the Gila River, bartering with the Indians along the way. Franz kept a diary and also began compiling a dictionary of the Apache language. The guide got them lost in the White Mountains on the return, and the entire party suffered greatly from frostbite and starvation.

They arrived at the Indian pueblo of Zuni more dead than alive. The native governor found them quarters and took up a collection of food, which proved their salvation. Some U.S. soldiers on duty there, however, stole all the traders' possessions while they slept, including Franz's diary and hard won dictionary.

Back on the Rio Grande Franz Huning became the legal secretary and interpreter for Federal Judge Kirby Benedict. The rotund judge was famous for riding circuit clad in a flowered chintz dressing gown. He loved liquor and poker, and thought nothing of stacking the deck. Franz saved the judge's life one night when he hid the six-shooter of a player who had been cheated and was ready to commit murder.

In 1857 Franz settled in Albuquerque and opened a small store on the plaza. He soon added a flour mill to his business and that was the beginning of his prosperity. Each year he led his own ox caravan back to Missouri to buy merchandise at wholesale, eventually making a total of forty trips across the plains.

He was in St. Louis on one of those ventures in 1862 when news arrived that Confederates from El Paso had ascended the Rio Grande and seized Albuquerque and Santa Fe. Franz was fearful that his store would be looted by the rebel army but happily it escaped unscathed. But his residence was taken for use by Confederate officers.

After the war his growing wealth led him to become a pillar of the community. He also played a prominent role in a local cell of vigilantes. In one instance he headed masked citizens who grabbed three outlaws from a saloon and hanged them from a tree in front of the flour mill.

After the railroad came in 1880 and he had added to his fortune through canny real estate deals, Franz decided to build himself a mansion. In fact, he built a castle, like those on the Rhine he had seen in his native Germany. The Castle Huning, as it was known, with its acres of European-style gardens became a landmark pointed out to visitors.

When he was seventy Franz's flour mill burned down. That was the last part of his old business he still retained. Standing sadly viewing the smoking ashes, he announced that he would not be living much longer. Soon after he took to his bed and died.

His Castle Huning survived until 1955 when it was finally torn down by a wrecking crew. A more enduring legacy, however, can be noted in two of his grandchildren who became popular Southwestern authors. Novelist Harvey Fergusson and historian-travel writer Erna Fergusson often claimed that the pioneer heritage bequeathed by Franz left a permanent imprint on their lives and work.

The Huning Castle, Albuquerque (Museum of Albuquerque photograph)

Physicians in the late Territorial period had little in the way of medicines or equipment

DOCTORING IN BERNALILLO

IN 1879 YOUNG DOCTOR HENRY HOYT was a practicing physician in Las Vegas, New Mexico. Competition was keen there—too many doctors in one town—so when he heard of an opportunity at Bernalillo over on the Rio Grande, he decided to move.

Bernalillo's only physician was a Dr. Carroll who was old and about to retire. Further, the place had no drugstore. So, Hoyt decided to open one, a common practice among frontier doctors eager to supplement their meager incomes.

Before leaving Las Vegas the youthful Hoyt approached the owner of the town's largest drugstore and asked for a grubstake—$2,000 worth of drugs that he could take to Bernalillo. They were immediately given.

"And you'll need some start up money," said the owner. So he casually peeled off $200 in cash from a large roll.

"In this transaction," wrote Hoyt afterward in his memoirs, "there wasn't a scratch of pen between us, simply a gentleman's agreement and a hand shake. That was the West in those days!"

Dr. Hoyt rode to Bernalillo in a buckboard, sending his medicines by ox train. Soon after his arrival he fell ill with a severe fever.

Old Dr. Carroll was called in to attend him. "He at once confided in me that he was not a real physician; that all he ever gave was quinine, castor oil, and native wine. This fine wine was made from the famous Mission grapes that are found everywhere in the Rio Grande Valley, from Bernalillo to El Paso."

Whether it was the wine or the castor oil, Hoyt soon recovered and was ready to practice medicine on his own. His first call came one midnight.

A native woman, in dreadful pain for twenty-four hours, had not been helped by Dr. Carroll's attentions. Therefore, the family decided to try the new doctor in town. Hoyt discovered the patient was suffering from an acute bladder infection and he was able to provide her quick relief. "From that night on," he said, "my reputation in Bernalillo was on a firm basis."

Another case soon increased his standing. A prominent citizen, Don José Montoya was down with double pneumonia. Dr. Carroll had informed his relatives that there was no hope, and then he left town for Santa Fe.

Related Hoyt, "A son-in-law of the patient asked me to come and stay at the house and let them know just before the end that they might have a priest perform the last rites. I agreed on the condition that I be given charge of the case."

Entering the sick room the doctor found that, as was usual, every window and door was tightly closed. New Mexicans in those days believed that fresh air meant instant death for the ailing. In addition, the place was packed with relatives. "The Montoya clan was a large one," remembered Hoyt, "and I think every one of them was there."

"In the face of strong protests, I threw open all windows, put on extra blankets, and had the bed moved so that Don José's head was near the window with the most air. A daughter acted as nurse applying the remedies I had ordered."

Shortly the patient reached a crises and coughed up matter from his lungs. This caused him to choke and he grew black in the face. Don José's wife screamed, "*El es muerto!* (He is dead!)" and promptly fainted, as did two other women.

Dr. Hoyt leaped into action. "Throwing aside the women who had fainted, I quickly rolled the old man on his stomach, pulled his head back by grabbing a handful of hair, then I jerked his lower jaw open, pulled his tongue out, and shook his head vigorously to clear his throat."

"This treatment I kept up for a minute or two, the breathing returned as did the color, and in a short time Don José was resting easily. Eventually he recovered."

Later, Dr. Hoyt submitted his bill—$500 in gold. He heard that while Don José had been counting out the sum, the priest had dropped by. "You are paying the doctor too much," remarked the clergyman.

"He saved my life," replied the Don. "I would have gladly paid him twice as much if he had asked it."

Once an epidemic of mumps broke out among the poor people of Bernalillo. Hoyt recommended that beans be used as a poultice to draw out the swelling. Hearing reports that the remedy was not working, he went to investigate. To his surprise, he found that each suffering child had a cloth bag of dried beans tied to his jaw!

Often the doctor was required to make long rides into the country to some outlying ranch or sheep camp to set a broken arm or leg. Ordinarily, no materials were available that he could use as splints. In the emergency, Hoyt tells us, "I would order a panful of adobe mud and use it exactly as we use plaster of Paris. I had fine results with it."

His story reminds me of an incident I heard about several years ago. A Navajo came into Albuquerque and bought a car off a dealer's lot for $300, partly on credit. Within a few days the radiator sprang a dozen leaks. After unsuccessful attempts at repair, it was left abandoned behind the Navajo's hogan.

Eventually, the dealer came to the reservation to collect his car, since payments had stopped. Raising the hood, he discovered that the radiator was packed entirely with dried adobe mud!

Solomon Luna

THE STRANGE END OF 'KING SAUL'

IN THE EARLY 20TH CENTURY few men were better known in New Mexico or wielded more political power than Republican leader Solomon Luna. Family and close friends called him Sol, but his Democrat foes, with clenched teeth, used another name, 'King Saul.'

Solomon, born in Los Lunas in 1858, came from an upper class family with roots extending to the mid colonial period. His father, Antonio José Luna, a wealthy sheep baron, provided tutors and then sent him to St. Louis University where the young man received his degree.

Returning home, Solomon with his older brother Tranquilino settled into management of the vast family properties. The symbol of their influence in Valencia County was the Luna mansion on Main Street in Los Lunas.

Back in 1881, the advancing Santa Fe Railroad had acquired a right of way from their father in exchange for building the Lunas a new house. Company officials gave the dynamic Isabel Baca Luna, the boys' mother, a railway pass so that she could travel in the Deep South and select an architectural style that appealed to her.

What eventually appeared on the dusty Los Lunas street was a white two-story Victorian mansion in the style of a Southern plantation. Hidden under the veneer, however, were walls of adobe brick.

Tranquilino Luna, a New Mexico territorial delegate to Congress, died prematurely in 1892. Solomon thereupon became head of the family, and about the same time emerged as a force in the Republican Party. In 1896 he was chosen a member of the National Republican Committee.

Luna ruled Valencia County as its *patrón*, or political boss. But as Albuquerque surged ahead, he increasingly spent time there, diversifying his financial interests.

Soon he was vice president of the First National Bank, an officer of the Occidental Life Insurance Company, and a player in local real estate development. A high-tone subdivision on New York Avenue (now Lomas Boulevard) was named Luna Place.

In 1903 Solomon accompanied his friend Governor Miguel A. Otero to Washington, lobbying the White House on behalf of New Mexico statehood. The territorial press lionized him as a millionaire banker, a model of virtue, and a public benefactor.

There was a dark side to Luna's reputation, nevertheless. Political opponents accused him of "voting the sheep" in his county. That meant giving names to each sheep in a flock and using them on ballots going into the election box. It was then a common practice in New Mexico.

Another source claimed that Luna was not smart enough to concoct these gigantic thefts of votes, but was put up to it by "the Santa Fe Ring, the real machine controlling the political situation in New Mexico."

To escape the stresses of politics in Albuquerque and Santa Fe, Solomon Luna enjoyed visiting his far flung ranches. During the last week of August, 1912, he inspected his operation at Horse Springs, southwest of Magdalena.

The ranch house was a large adobe structure with an open courtyard, Spanish style. Behind the building stood a long narrow dipping vat filled with sheep dip made of water, tobacco, and lime to a depth of 3 ½ feet. Beyond the vat was the privy.

In the middle of the night, Luna arose to visit the privy. At 7:00 the next morning, an employee saw something strange floating in the vat. Taking a long pole with a hook, used to handle the sheep, he pulled the object to the edge. To his horror, it proved to be the body of his *patrón*, Solomon Luna.

The Santa Fe *New Mexican* in explaining the death said that Don Solomon apparently had stopped to wash his hands in the dark. The faucet was overhanging the vat and he must have fainted or suffered a heart attack, causing him to fall into the slimy liquid and drown.

Since Luna had enemies and assassinations were part of the political landscape, there were those who suggested that his death was not an accident. But no evidence ever surfaced to confirm that.

Still, it was an unusual and particularly grisly end for the influential and wealthy 'King Saul.'

Luna Mansion

VI

FOREVER, COWBOY

Llano Estacado Cowboys (National Archives photograph)

COWBOYS OF THE LLANO

THE HIGH, PANCAKE-FLAT PLATEAU that sprawls across eastern New Mexico and western Texas has long been known by the romantic name El Llano Estacado, or Staked Plains. Some historians of the frontier refer to it as one of the Old West's most mysterious and hostile environments.

As a region, it was among the last to defy the inroads of civilization. The vastness of the plains kept at bay all but the hardiest folk. Perhaps for that very reason, the Llano has always had a special appeal for me.

The original inhabitants were Apaches, at least that was the tribe Coronado found when he explored the heart of the Llano Estacado in 1541. He gets credit, too, for naming the area.

According to a popular story, these first Spaniards of the Coronado expedition were fearful of losing their way on the open plains without landmarks. So every half league they drove a wooden stake in the ground, marking their back trail and providing a way out.

Later, in the 18th century, the Comanches invaded the Llano, drove out the Apaches, and with their allies, the Kiowas, held ownership of the plains for 150 years. In that period, outsiders entered the region at their peril.

In the 1870s, two events changed the history of the Llano Estacado. One was the invasion of the hide hunters who in a few short years exterminated the great buffalo herds.

The second event was the war between the U.S. Army and the Indians. By 1875 the Comanches and Kiowas had been swept from the plains and banished to reservations in Oklahoma.

With the buffalo and the Indian gone, the day of the cattleman dawned. Men of daring, booted and spurred, drove cattle upon the plains and founded ranching empires that served as models for other sections of the West.

Initially, native New Mexican sheepmen surged eastward into portions of the newly opened land, building settlements as far as Tascosa in the Texas Panhandle. But the pressure of an expanding range cattle industry obliged most of them to withdraw into New Mexico.

The history of Hispano ranching on the Llano has been delightfully told in the classic little book, *We Fed Them Cactus*, by Santa Fe author Fabiola Cabeza de Vaca (who died at age 97). First published in 1954, it remains in print today and is must-reading for Southwestern aficionados.

Among all the denizens through time on the Llano Estacado, it was the rancher and cowboy who were to leave the strongest mark on the history and folklore of the country. They would be succeeded largely, though not entirely, by modern irrigation farmers, but a vestige of the original "cowboy culture" is still preserved there with affection.

In 1947, old-time cowman Billy Dodson who had ranched on the Llano back in the wild days gave a speech telling what it was like. Fortunately, he wrote down his remarks and they were preserved.

"One of my cowpunchers," he said, "once joked that the Llano Estacado was the most convenient country he'd ever lived in. Here, wind drew the water and the cows chopped the wood. He had reference, of course, to our windmills and to the fact that in the absence of trees we had to use dried cow chips for fuel."

Dodson claimed that the Llano was then a man's world and no place for a woman. "For more than a year and a half," he quipped, "I never even saw a woman and I wasn't in jail either. The few women were idolized by the men, they would ride miles just to see a woman's face again, and woe unto anyone who offended her."

Many people later became misinformed as to the real character of the Llano's ranchers and cowboys, Billy Dodson believed. He blamed that on Hollywood movies and pulp magazines that pictured range riders as ignorant, uncouth, and ready to shoot at the drop of a hat.

"Well, maybe some of our boys were not well versed in the finer arts one learned in school, but they were not ignorant," he insisted. "We even had a few high school graduates and college men, but they didn't hang their sheepskins on the chuck box."

Neither was the man of the open range a killer, at least in the modern sense of that term, contended Billy. The cowboy was usually a gentleman, but one quick to defend his honor or that of his family. On the Llano Estacado, such things were customarily settled between the individuals themselves.

"There was no law on the plains in those days," he reminisced. "But we rose to the occasion and formed our own Law of the Range. This code was never written down but still it was respected and efficiently administered."

Some of these unwritten laws mentioned by Dodson included: 1) Never abuse a horse; 2) Always help a man in need; 3) Be ready to defend all woman-kind; 4) Avoid eating stolen beef; 5) When receiving the hospitality of a meal, always offer to help with the dishes; and, 6) Camp robbing is an unpardonable offense and the guilty will be branded like a horse thief.

"It took men of vision and courage to settle the Llano Estacado," Billy Dodson said. "But we accepted the challenge and heart-breaking discouragements."

There is no reason to doubt either the truth of his words or his sincerity. Some of today's harsh critics of the settlement of the West would do well to pay attention.

Veteran cowboys like this one made life hard for greenhorns

A GREENHORN MAKES THE GRADE

ONE OF THE STOCK STORIES in the history of the Old West deals with the young eastern tenderfoot who decides to leave home and go out to the big ranch country to become a cowboy. During his apprenticeship he undergoes a difficult transformation from inept sissy to a competent cowhand.

The theme occurs repeatedly in western literature. Author and artist Will James made frequent use of it in his popular books on cowboy life.

A good example can be found in the case of A.B. Wadleigh who first came to New Mexico in 1886 during the boom days of the open range. He'd grown up in the East, but reading books on the West convinced him that's where his future lay.

When he was 16, he learned that a friend of the family had bought a cow ranch in New Mexico. Remarks Wadleigh in his memoirs, "After much persuasion my mother gave her consent to my starting out. I was pretty strong and husky for my age. What a grand time I had buying my outfit: flannel shirts, a 44 Winchester, and a 45 Colt revolver."

In April he departed by rail for the six day trip. Beyond Kansas City, he says, "I had my eyes glued to the car window. Everything was new and different. At last I was in the real West that I had read and dreamed about."

After a brief stop in Albuquerque, he continued down the Rio Grande to Socorro, the end of his railroad journey. There he bought a raw-boned buckskin horse and a used saddle for $75. Then he started for Magdalena, thirty miles to the west by a rough trail.

Late that night, dead tired, he rode into town and had to be lifted out of the saddle and put to bed. "I doubt whether many other kids, who had been brought up as I was, would ever have made the trip," he comments wryly.

Of Magdalena, he says that it was not much of a town to look at in 1886—a dozen houses, five or six saloons, a hotel and general store. "But it was the shipping and distributing point for an enormous country to the west. And it was tough because the country was tough. Everyone went armed. You were not dressed without a belt full of cartridges and a six shooter."

Later Wadleigh made his way south over the San Mateo Mountains to his job at the C Bar N ranch. The crude headquarters was fortified in case of Apache attack, and there were no beds. The cowhands spread their blankets on the floor. The food, he found, was equally spartan: coffee, sourdough bread, sow belly, beans, and potatoes, and once in a while canned tomatoes as a special treat.

Soon after his arrival he was given a sleepy looking horse to ride. But it was one reserved especially for greenhorns. Once in the saddle the rider found that he was on top of a bucking volcano.

"I got into the saddle," he reported, "but was immediately thrown. After five attempts I managed to stick it out. I was pretty well shaken up but I made up my mind that I would show I had the nerve to stay with it. Of course this all furnished much amusement for the boys!"

With this display of gumption the young man, in one stroke, won his spurs. No longer was he regarded as a tenderfoot to be made fun of.

During the next several years he lived the high, dangerous life of a cowboy on the open range. There were trail drives, lonely winter vigils in an isolated line camp, round-ups, and even a cattle stampede.

"I remember one night, dark and stormy, when there was a stampede. The herd ran straight for camp. The cook had a hard time saving himself as the cattle ran through his fire scattering pots and pans and grub all over the landscape. Only one who has been through a stampede knows what a wild and thrilling thing it is."

Late in life as he was setting down his recollections, Wadleigh reflected upon the meaning of his early cowboy adventures. "I looked back to those days with the greatest pleasure and am proud of the fact that I helped to build up the country. I am glad I was there to have seen the Great Southwest when men were men and the incentive to do and see were not softened, when travel was not easy and when life was hard. I think of the days gone by, with their primitive pleasures, their hardships, and above all their joy of living."

A.B. Wadleigh wrote those words in the early 1950s when he was 82 and in retirement in Tucson. The rosy memory of his youth spent on the New Mexico range appears to have been something that he savored in his final years.

Cowboys branding cattle on New Mexico's eastern plains

A TEENAGER'S RITE OF PASSAGE

IN 1885 CHARLES POPE WAS FIFTEEN YEARS OLD, living in a large city of the Midwest. His father, a prominent physician, moved in the best social circles and provided the family all the desirable luxuries.

"In that year my parents became concerned," Charles would say later, "because I was under weight and not very strong for my age. Believing my health would benefit by a summer in the open air, they arranged to send me to a ranch in New Mexico, as the guest of an old family friend."

That friend was Doctor Edward Enriques, of French descent from Michigan and a former colleague of Doctor Pope. In the late 1870s, he had taken a job as company doctor for the Santa Fe Railroad, but shortly after being assigned to Las Vegas, New Mexico, he resigned the position.

The reason was, he had met and married in that town a beautiful lady of Hispanic descent. Her family owned extensive ranching properties throughout the Territory, which were managed by her brother.

It was to one of the cattle ranches, belonging to Doctor Enriques' in-laws, that fifteen year old Charles would be sent. Said he, "To a city bred boy whose mind was full of secret longings to be a cowboy and who was tired of school, it proved a fascinating prospect."

He arrived in Las Vegas and was shown the local sights by Enriques and his wife. Then he and the doctor boarded the train and rode it to Belen on the Rio Grande, where they obtained a buckboard and matched team of driving horses.

In the next three days, they crossed Abo Pass and descended upon New Mexico's eastern plains. Finally, the boy and the doctor arrived at the family's largest and most isolated ranch, whose headquarters sat next to a gushing spring.

Since Enriques was a member of the owners' family, the foreman and hands all turned out to give him a respectful greeting. He explained that he had come to observe the annual branding, but also to deliver into their care young Charles Pope.

The wide-eyed boy saw that the main ranch house was an old rambling structure with thick adobe walls, built with two wings, like the letter U. The foreman and his wife occupied one wing and the hired hands the other.

But it was the colorful cowboys, half of them young Texans and the rest young New Mexicans, that engaged Charles' avid attention. In his eyes, they were true storybook characters.

"These cowboys were superb horsemen and experts with a rope," he wrote. "A few wore chaps and spurs, but their boots, worn down at the heels, were never polished. They seldom shaved. And only on long rides did they carry a holstered gun."

Dr. Enriques soon returned to Las Vegas, leaving Charles in the custody of the foreman. Unknowingly, he was also giving the cowboys an opportunity to have some fun with the green Eastern boy who was still wet behind the ears.

"I was a heaven sent victim for their rough practical jokes," Charles commented. "They wanted to test me to see if I was a sissy or a lad with enough courage to take whatever they gave me without whimpering."

One afternoon with the foreman gone, the cowboys seized their chance and asked Charles whether he wouldn't like to ride a gentle horse they had in the corral. He innocently agreed.

The boy was so eager and gullible that he failed to notice the snickers of the men, especially when he neglected to test the saddle cinch and then mounted on the wrong side.

Once he was on board, the horse began to spin around like a top and he promptly lost his stirrups. They banged against the animal's sides, causing it to bolt out the gate, carelessly left open, and go streaking across the prairie.

The cowboys were thunderstruck. They had expected the lad to be thrown off instantly in the soft dirt of the corral. Now on a runaway, he was in serious danger. They quickly mounted up and went in pursuit.

They had a long chase, since the bronco with the boy clinging to his back ran several miles before exhaustion forced him to stop of his own accord. Riding up, they asked Charles if he had been scared.

"When I truthfully told them I had enjoyed the ride and was not frightened, they were astonished. I'd done everything wrong, but perhaps I was a real rider and had turned the tables on them."

That evening the foreman learned what had happened and was so angry he prepared to fire some of the cowboys. But Charles defended them and said it had only been a joke.

When the boys heard he had not complained and had taken their part, as Charles put it, "from then on I was one of them."

At summer's end, heading home, the teenager realized he had been granted a rare opportunity to experience authentic range life. Growing up to become a successful business man, he never came west again. But he never forgot that one memorable experience.

A pair of cowboys, one tall and one short, proudly pose with their ropes

THOSE COWBOYS WITH ROPES

IN THE OLD WEST every range-riding cowboy carried a catch rope tied to his saddle. And he knew how to use it, even though roping was one of the most difficult ranch skills to learn.

Young boys raised in cattle country had a rope placed in their hands almost as soon as they could walk. For practice, they would toss a loop over anything that moved, from chickens to a baby sister.

Cowboys considered a good rope one of their most useful tools. From horseback, calves could be caught by head or heels and dragged to the branding fire, or a cow pulled from a mud bog.

On foot, men would enter a corral at sunup and using a throw called the hoolihan catch a riding horse needed for the day's work. Often the ranch had a star roper who performed this chore for the rest of the crew.

Most cowboys could rope fairly well. But only a few showed natural talent and spectacular skill. In range parlance, such men were said to be, "as scarce as bird dung in a cuckoo clock."

When the opportunity to make a difficult catch presented itself, no red-blooded roper could let the challenge go by. The *Silver City Enterprise* in 1893 reported an example for its readers.

The newspaper ran its story under the headline, "Cowboy Goodin Ropes a Lion." Doc Goodin was identified as the person who recently broke the world's record at steer-tying in 48 seconds.

It seems he had been riding down a steep trail when he and his horse came face to face with a mountain lion. Both parties were startled by the encounter, but Goodin recovered first.

By instinct, he grabbed his catch rope and shook out a loop. Then putting spurs to his mount he charged straight for Mr. Lion.

The loop sailed through the air with considerable force and landed true, around the furry throat. Said the *Enterprise*, in graphic terms, "The cougar made a desperate fight, but the skillful cowboy managed to run his horse on one side of a mesquite tree and the ferocious animal on the other."

As a result of this maneuver, the mountain lion broke its neck and was left hanging in the tree. Cowboy Goodin lifted the scalp and brought it in to collect the bounty.

The roping of wild life in those days, as much for sport as anything else, was not all that uncommon—lions, wildcats, bears, buffalo, deer, and elk. Now, of course, it is a practice justifiably frowned upon.

In old California, during the days before the American conquest, Mexican vaqueros were in the habit of roping grizzly bears for entertainment. It was a dangerous way to have fun.

A band of them would surround a bear and cast their *reatas* upon the neck and legs to capture it. These ropes were made of four strands of rawhide braided together, and were both strong and beautiful.

At a fiesta, a grizzly and a bull were sometimes placed in arena and tied together by a rope with plenty of slack. The animals were baited so they would fight to the death in a very gory spectacle.

Nothing like that occurred in New Mexico, so far as we know. But Santa Fe trader Josiah Gregg in 1844 reported that vaqueros here did rope bears and lions.

The use of the *lazo*, says Gregg, was not confined to vaqueros and mule skinners, since no rural man considered his education complete "until he had mastered this national accomplishment."

Nowadays, roping is seen less and less on the open range, because modern methods and equipment are tending to displace it. The mechanical squeeze chute, for instance, is a handy device for holding an animal in need of doctoring or branding.

But roping survives as a sport or as a profession in competitive rodeo. Because of specialization and intensive practice, the calf ropers and steer ropers of today are far faster and more proficient than the regular cowboys of a century ago.

The catch rope, the ten-gallon hat, and a pair of spurs remain as recognizable symbols of the old-style cowboy life that is now all but gone.

Black Cowboy George McJunkin (Museum of New Mexico photograph)

McJUNKIN FINDS SOME BONES

THE HISTORY OF ARCHAEOLOGY in the Southwest owes a great debt to a black cowboy named George McJunkin. While riding the range near Clayton in the northeast corner of New Mexico, he found some prehistoric bison bones that in the 1920s helped scholars unravel the mystery of the earliest Indians in North America.

George was born a slave in central Texas about the year 1855. All around him were big ranches and close to his family's home cattle drives passed by on their way north. As far back as he could remember, he wanted to be a cowboy. But his father tried to discourage him. White cowboys, he said, were not apt to admit a black youngster to their clannish ranks.

George McJunkin, however, was a determined lad. He knew what he wanted. So two years after the Civil War ended, when he was seventeen, he climbed on a mule and headed out.

With a little luck, he landed a job as a horse wrangler and cook's helper with a trail drive. On the long trip to Dodge City, he watched the regular cowboys closely and learned all he could from them. By the time the drive was over, George had mastered most of the tricks of the cow trade.

Back in Texas, he went looking for ranch work, but openings for blacks were scarce just as his daddy had predicted. Nevertheless, he was soon hired by a mustanger, a man who took a crew onto the

Staked Plains to capture wild horses. George was a good bronc rider and went along to break the mustangs the other men brought in.

After a winter in Palo Duro Canyon, the mustanger and his men moved west into New Mexico. George liked the people and the country below the Raton Mesa and he soon had a steady job on the Pitchfork Ranch. Here on the plains of eastern New Mexico he was to remain the rest of his life.

The next spring, the boss of the neighboring Crowfoot Ranch rode over and offered him a job—not as a cowboy but as foreman of the ranch. George jumped at the chance, even though he was a little nervous. He didn't know what to expect from the dozen white cowboys who would be working under him. But he need not have worried. Nobody let out a peep. They knew George McJunkin was a man to be respected, a top hand who had won his spurs.

Years passed and George became a permanent fixture at the Crowfoot. Men left to look for new jobs and some cowboys died, but always he stayed on. One day in the early part of this century, he went looking for strays below the little town of Folsom. Riding down Wild Horse Arroyo, he spotted a curious bone eroding out of the bank. George dismounted and pulled it free from the dirt. It was the largest bone he had ever seen.

George McJunkin was uneducated but he had a natural curiosity. He carried the bone back to the Crowfoot bunkhouse and put it on the mantelpiece. None of the cowboys knew what it was or seemed to care. But George cared and he wanted to know.

Many times he went back to the arroyo to find more bones. He referred to the place as his Bone Pit. The other hands began to tease him for wasting time there. In the early 1920s, he rode to Raton forty miles west to have a small job done at the blacksmith shop. On the walls George was surprised to see deer and elk antlers—and bones. The smith, it seems, was also a collector.

George told him about his own finds out in Wild Horse Arroyo and he invited the smith to come and see them. The man expressed interest, but before they could plan a trip George McJunkin died, on January 21, 1922.

Some months later, the smith went to Wild Horse Arroyo and found George's Bone Pit. Collecting a bag full of specimens, he carried them home, deposited them in a corner and forgot all about the matter. Five years went by. The local banker stopped in the blacksmith shop one day. He was interested in science and wanted to see all the old bones the smith had accumulated.

The bag from the Bone Pit was pulled out, the banker took one look, and knew that here was something rare. On his next business trip to Denver, he carried several samples to show to officials at the Colorado Museum of Natural History. They identified the bones as coming from the giant prehistoric bison that had roamed the plains 8000 years ago.

An expedition was fitted out and scholars began to dig at the Bone Pit. In the course of the work, they unearthed something wholly unexpected. Lodged between the ribs of a bison skeleton was a beautiful stone dart point. Some ancient Indian hunter had killed the animal and left this evidence behind. It was the first definite proof that Indians had inhabited the plains far back in the prehistoric period. Archaeologists from everywhere, including the Smithsonian Institution, came to view the site. Other dart points were found and they called them Folsom points.

In all fairness, the artifacts should have been named "McJunkin points" in honor of the black cowboy who helped bring about one of the most significant discoveries in American archaeology.

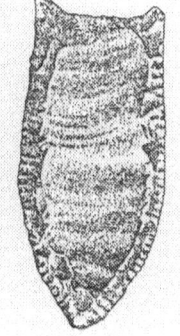

Folsom Point

Charlie Siringo as a young cowboy (r.) (Plate from *A Texas Cowboy*)

THE COWBOY DETECTIVE

FOR A NUMBER OF YEARS prior to 1922, one of Santa Fe's most colorful and famous residents was Charles A. Siringo, popularly known as "the cowboy detective." A small, wiry man, he was friends with practically everyone in town, from the governor to the dog catcher.

In 1916 Governor William C. McDonald persuaded Siringo to accept a commission as a New Mexico Mounted Ranger for the state Cattle Sanitary Board. The only thing unusual about that was Charlie Siringo's age, a ripe 61. Undaunted, he saddled up and with a pack horse, he started for his headquarters at Carrizozo in Lincoln County.

His duty was to run down outlaws and stock thieves in southern New Mexico. Bill Owens, described as a fighting son-of-a-gun, became his partner. As Siringo reported later, "Poor Bill lasted only a short time."

The pair got into a gun fight with cattle thieves at Abo Pass east of Belen. Owens was shot through the lungs, but he emptied his pistol and killed two of the outlaws before he went down.

"During my two years as a ranger," said Siringo, "I made many arrests of cattle and horse thieves and had many close calls with death staring me in the face." Obviously, Governor McDonald had made a wise choice when he tapped this hard-riding, fast-shooting "senior citizen" for the dangerous ranger job.

Charlie Siringo's career in the West was as adventurous as it was long. Raised in Matagorda County, Texas, he took to life in the saddle before he was shaving.

As he put it, "When I was twelve years of age, in the spring of 1867, I became a full-fledged cowboy, wearing broad sombrero, high-heeled boots, Mexican spurs and the dignity of a full-grown man."

After trips up the Chisholm Trail, he landed a cowboy job in the Texas Panhandle, still a teenager. He fought prairie fires, had run-ins with rustlers and saw the last herds of buffalo roaming the Staked Plains.

The years drifted by and Charlie Siringo drifted with them. At age thirty he was tending store at Caldwell, Kansas and putting in nights writing up his previous experiences on the range.

When his book, *A Texas Cowboy*, appeared, its author achieved fame overnight. Eventually, it sold a million copies and to this day remains in print.

Soon after publishing his recollections, Siringo joined the renowned Pinkerton Detective Agency, whose branch offices covered the West. He remained with the firm for two decades, getting in and out of more scrapes than a modern TV sleuth.

The Pinkerton men first gained national attention just before the Civil War when they foiled a plot to assassinate Lincoln on the way to his inauguration. Later they made headlines in trying to break up Jesse James' gang, an effort that cost several detectives their lives.

Pinkertons were often hired as strike-breakers. They proved so successful that they earned the bitter hatred of organized unions. Siringo participated in one episode at Coeur d'Alene, Idaho.

There in 1892 occurred huge labor riots attended by the dynamiting of mines and the murder of managers. In trials that followed, Agent Siringo gave crucial testimony that led to the conviction of eighteen union leaders for these crimes. Soon afterward, the home office sent him in pursuit of Butch Cassidy's Wild Bunch.

After leaving the Pinkertons, Charlie Siringo returned to the Southwest and did a good bit of roaming before settling in Santa Fe.

Because of the name he'd made in publishing *A Texas Cowboy*, he had access to many persons, on both sides of the law, who were on their way to winning a place in the history books. From them he got first hand information that he later incorporated in a new book called *Riata and Spurs*.

In that work, the writer had wanted to include some of his own daring adventures while serving with the Pinkertons. But the Agency threatened a lawsuit if he revealed any of their professional secrets. So the cowboy detective had to delete some of his best material.

There is a prominent thoroughfare in Santa Fe today called Siringo Road. But it is a safe guess that not one local resident in 500 knows for whom it is named.

VII

ITINERANT WRITERS

Street Scene in Old Santa Fe, 1870s

"GO WEST, YOUNG MAN"

IN 1868 JOHN H. BEADLE was a young lawyer with a serious medical problem. A confirmed asthmatic, he was wracked by "an ominous graveyard cough." At home in Evansville, Indiana, he says that he was the despair of his mother and friends, and the worry of his creditors who feared he would die before paying his bills.

In those days, when all else failed, invalids were urged to travel, in the hope that a change of environment might work a cure. Since a score of nasty cough syrups in villainous green bottles had done him no good, Beadle decided to try the travel treatment.

After selling all his law books and other possessions to pay off the debts, he was left with a paltry $115. Since that wouldn't take him very far, he signed on with the Cincinnati Commercial as a correspondent. Articles submitted to the paper in the course of his journey allowed him to cover expenses.

But where to go? Some well-meaning friends suggested a long sea voyage. Others argued for a leisurely road trip to Florida. But it was Beadle's own doctor who decided the issue. "Go West, young man," he advised, "Go West!"

Initially, the health-seeker plotted a route that would take him through all the western territories and states, a circuit, he figured, that would require about two years to complete. In the end his wanderings took him more than twice that long. And, out of them came a book, published in 1873, titled *The Undeveloped West; or, Five Years in the Territories.*

Luckily, Beadle's itinerary included New Mexico. From his brief tour comes some amusing and insightful observations of life along the Rio Grande in the early 1870s. Reaching Santa Fe by stagecoach from Denver, he found the capital a delightful place, filled with astonishing Old World sights.

Everywhere strings of loaded burros caught his eye. Many were piled high with firewood and when one occasionally lost his balance and went over on its back, it was helpless, like an upturned insect. One day Beadle saw a tiny donkey, no bigger than a ram, transporting an entire bedstead.

"The people of New Mexico are so polite," he reports, "that one rarely knows if he has made a mistake in speaking Spanish." The newcomer, no matter how wretched his pronunciation or grammar, was constantly showered with compliments on his "clear Castilian."

The young writer included an anecdote to illustrate the problems that sometimes arose over ignorance of language. It concerned a newly appointed federal official who came to Santa Fe having learned a few Spanish phrases, which he thought sufficient to get him through ordinary business.

"Entering a restaurant," relates Beadle, "the official did not know what to order. At length he saw on the wall a rude picture of a dove, representing the Holy Spirit, such as is common in Catholic countries. He took this to be a sign for some game fowl, and asked, 'Como se llama eso?' (What is that?)"

"Un Espiritu Santo, Señor," (A Holy Spirit, Sir), replied the waiter.

"Pues, da me dos Espiritu Santos, bien cocidos," (Give me two Holy Spirits, well done) requested the official, to the great horror of the devout waiter.

Young Beadle was amazed to see the transformations that English names underwent in Spanish. A Mr. Meadows who had taken up local residence became Señor Las Vegas, while a Jim Gibbons was soon known as Don Santiago Gibbonoise. An Irishman he met who had settled at El Paso was originally named Tim

Murphy. But now, Beadle noted, he signed his checks grandly as Timotheus Murfando.

From Santa Fe, the traveler headed south on the stage, his health improving by the day. His first glimpse of the Rio Grande was disappointing for owing to the silt, "the waters were too thick to swim in."

Approaching the outskirts of Albuquerque, he described it as a great farming oasis. "The Valley of the Rio Grande here is as productive as the Valley of the Nile." And he added that "all the important towns are along the river, and one may ride from El Paso to Taos through a continuous line of settlements, while to cross the country from east to west, he will often travel for days without sight of a dwelling."

At Albuquerque Beadle crossed the Rio Grande on a crude ferry boat one Sunday morning. The other passengers on their way to Mass, continually shouted directions at the oarsman. The American declared, "A boat load of New Mexicans on their way to church can make more noise than two circus shows."

John Beadle crossed central New Mexico to Fort Wingate and then continued on to Fort Defiance just beyond the Arizona line. That was the beginning of a long excursion through the Navajo and Hopi country.

Beadle's book was never reprinted and so today only a few larger libraries have a copy. But it is worth looking for, since it provides an interesting glimpse of what one observant person discovered when he took the advice of his doctor to "Go West, young man!"

George W. Kendall

A REMARKABLE NEWSPAPERMAN

CHARLES BENNETT, HISTORIAN FOR THE MUSEUM of New Mexico, sent me some material on frontier journalist George Wilkins Kendall. "If you haven't dealt with him before, he might be worth a write-up," he suggested.

Kendall, indeed, is an interesting historical figure, one whose name today is unfamiliar to most Southwesterners. But in the 1840s, he was known around the country.

Born in New Hampshire in 1809, the same year Kit Carson was born in Kentucky, Kendall started out as a printer. Graduating to news reporter, he worked briefly at the *New York Tribune* for Horace Greeley.

Young George Kendall went southwest to New Orleans in 1837 where with $400 he founded the *Picayune*, destined to become one of the most celebrated newspapers of its day.

The word picayune, incidentally, referred to a dime-size silver coin worth about six cents, equal to a Spanish half real. That was the price of the paper.

Kendall gave extended coverage in his paper to happenings in the newly established Republic of Texas, a country for which he developed a special fondness. That affection led him to join the disastrous Texan-Santa Fe Expedition of 1841.

Texas President Mirabeau B. Lamar launched the expedition in a bid to open commerce with New Mexico. Thinking that a worthy goal, Kendall signed on as a U.S. news correspondent to cover the event.

After becoming lost on the plains, the 320-man expedition reached New Mexico in a starving condition. Governor Manuel Armijo at Santa Fe chose to regard it as a hostile invasion, and he placed the Texans under arrest.

George Kendall, although a U.S. citizen and carrying a passport issued by the Mexican Consul in New Orleans, was treated like the rest. As he would write about it later, what occurred next was like a chamber of horrors.

Armijo decided to send his prisoners on a 1,500 mile march to a lock-up in Mexico City. Over them he placed Captain Damasio Salazar, remembered now as one of the supreme villains of New Mexico history.

As the Texans trudged down the Rio Grande Valley, the sick and weak fell out of line and Salazar ordered them shot at trailside. He then cut off their ears to take back to Armijo, as proof that none had escaped.

The fear, misery, and hunger lasted as far as El Paso where the prisoner's situation brightened considerably. As Kendall put it, "Upon entering this beautiful and romantic city, our feelings were impossible to describe, ... for we hoped to fall into kinder hands."

And so they did. The Commandant General José Elias González was indignant when he learned of the harsh treatment imposed by Salazar, whom he dismissed at once. The men were then fed, bathed, rested and given new clothes.

Kendall gave the General high praise, referring to him as "a well-bred, liberal, and gentlemanly officer."

The company eventually reached a prison in Mexico City where the journalist contracted small pox and almost died. Released in 1842, he made his way back to New Orleans to discover that owing to his captivity he had become a national celebrity.

Kendall published his experiences serially in the pages of the *Picayune*, which added to his fame. Then in 1844 he brought out his book in two volumes titled *Narrative of the Texan-Santa Fe Expedition*. It sold 40,000 copies.

Two years later war broke out between the United States and Mexico. Some historians claim that Kendall's book, with its description of Salazar's cruelties, helped inflame public opinion and thus contributed to the conflict.

Kendall himself immediately headed for Mexico with the American army to act as a war correspondent. He appears to have been the first person in history to fill that capacity.

His battlefield dispatches he rushed to New Orleans for publication and from the pages of the *Picayune* they were picked up by eastern papers. Often Washington officials read Kendall's account of major war events before they had gotten any notice of them from the army.

At the Battle of Monterrey, the journalist got caught up in the fighting. He even managed to capture a Mexican flag, which he sent back to New Orleans, where it was displayed for many years in the *Picayune* building.

After the war, Kendall retired to a ranch in Texas, dying there of yellow fever in 1867.

Albert D. Richardson (From *Beyond the Mississippi*)

AMBLING IN THE SOUTHWEST

ALBERT D. RICHARDSON LED AN EXCITING LIFE and suffered a tragic death. A century ago, most Americans knew his name, mainly because of the three books he wrote. Today, he is all but forgotten and his writings, never reprinted, gather dust in their old bindings on a few library shelves.

A native of Massachusetts, Richardson was born with a love of adventure and travel. Journalism became his chosen career, and from a position on a succession of eastern papers he angled several reporting trips that allowed him to visit the far corners of the Wild West.

Early in 1859, at age 25, Richardson crossed Kansas to write up the Pike's Peak gold discovery. By chance, one of his fellow passengers was the publisher of the *New York Tribune*, the famed Horace Greeley. A year later Greeley would offer him a good position on his paper.

Later in 1859, Richardson, having returned to St. Louis, caught the Butterfield Overland Stage for El Paso. He planned to survey New Mexico from bottom to top, and include his experiences in a book he was writing called *Beyond the Mississippi*.

After a grueling trip across Texas, by way of Horsehead Crossing on the Pecos, the journalist eagerly descended into the El Paso Valley. The town held 400 inhabitants, he found, and the prevailing language was Spanish.

His stage driver had advised him that if he wished to become a celebrity in this country, all he had to do was kill somebody. But Richardson's only interest was in observing the strange people and customs of the Southwest.

"Of narrow streets through which Mexican carts creak and rumble, half-naked boys bear water-kegs suspended from poles between them, women balance huge jars upon their heads, and little donkeys stagger under enormous loads."

To his New England eyes, it all appeared quite exotic. That included a fandango, where "the dancers' faces, lighted by tallow candles, made up a medley of hues from dark Indian to fairest Saxon."

At Mesilla, the first New Mexican town of importance above El Paso, Richardson saw the local judiciary in action. A tobacco-chewing Kentuckian, brought before the *alcalde* (judge) on a minor charge, was told to hire an interpreter to translate his words into Spanish for the court.

The defendant became irate and shouted that "the United States language ought to serve here!" And brandishing a revolver, he made his escape.

The journalist was now riding the weekly mail stagecoach that ascended the Rio Grande to Santa Fe. In the desert south of Socorro, he noted a rough wooden cross at trailside, where a violent death had occurred.

"Passing travelers," he was told, "each add a stone to the pile at its foot, helping to form a rude monument." It was another of the curious customs of the region.

Finally, Richardson reached the territorial capital at Santa Fe. He described it as the political and business metropolis, and the highest town of any size in the United States.

Visiting a jewelry shop on the plaza, he was horrified to see on display a necklace of human fingers, "collected by the Utes from Apaches they killed in war."

From here, the visitor returned east, going by way of Taos and Denver to avoid raiding Kiowas on the Santa Fe Trail. Because the Civil War soon erupted, the publication of the book containing his New Mexico experiences was delayed until 1867.

Two years after that he was murdered. Richardson, now a successful staff member of the *New York Tribune*, had been courting the beautiful Abby McFarland, who was recently divorced.

They had set a date for their wedding. But one week before, her jealous ex-husband entered the *Tribune*, and shot Richardson, wounding him fatally.

The journalist lingered for a week, during which he called for Abby and a preacher. Their deathbed marriage made national headlines.

In the final chapter of this soap opera, the killer, David McFarland, won acquittal at his trial through intervention of friends in the crooked Tammany Hall, a political ring.

Albert Richardson's *Beyond the Mississippi* is worth consulting, for those readers who want a glimpse of New Mexican life just before the Civil War.

A Busy Day in Santa Fe (contemporary engraving)

A JOURNALIST'S VISIT TO SANTA FE, 1875

TRAVELERS OF ALL KINDS found their way to Santa Fe in the years between 1850 and 1900—merchants, ox drivers, soldiers, clergymen, government men, gamblers, artists, tourists, railroaders, and yes, even a few journalists. Some of them left us their written impressions, both good and bad, of New Mexico's fair capital.

One was William H. Rideing, a cocky newspaperman from the East. He had been attached as a correspondent to the expedition of Lieutenant George M. Wheeler, who was charged with the survey and mapping of the western territories in the 1870s.

Part of that expedition, which had been working in eastern New Mexico, rode into Santa Fe to see what the storied place was all about. Rideing came along in hopes of finding some new and unusual material for his Atlantic seaboard readers.

On their approach, the journalist noted that his companions were speculating whether Santa Fe would shine like Paris or Rome, or whether it would turn out to be just another Pottsville. From his subsequent remarks, we gather that he judged it to be the latter.

The party entered town by what is today named Old Santa Fe Trail. Rideing reports that "it was a long narrow street lined with one-storied mud houses, built in the form of quadrangles with interior courtyards suggestive of small model prisons."

Through open doors he got a glimpse inside these "prisons" and he obtained a more favorable impression, as the inner rooms were clean and their walls freshly whitewashed. On the street, he observed ragged "hucksters seated at the corners selling their scant stocks of watermelons."

Our visitor passed what he described as "an old adobe church that is crumbling to ruin under the weight of 250 years." We suppose he was referring to San Miguel Chapel, today refurbished and touted in tourist advertising as the "Oldest Church."

The dirt street produced some odd and colorful sights. A Pueblo Indian trotted on a burro just ahead of the arriving Americans, who were astonished to see him riding on the animal's rump rather than up front.

At one point, a freight wagon drawn by eight oxen blocked the way. The New Mexican drivers "hissed and spluttered blasphemy," as they struggled to get the beasts in motion.

But finally the men reached the plaza where Rideing proclaimed that "all things looked foreign to us." He added "that in this small square with its leafy little park, we were at the very core of the Territory."

He and his companions took note of the Governor's Palace and thought it "completely uninteresting and unimaginably ugly." Evidently, the idea of "Santa Fe charm" had not yet occurred to Easterners.

And that was just the beginning of the journalist's criticisms. "In the park there is a Soldiers' Monument. It is an obelisk ... ungraceful and made by unskilled hands. The sculptor's name is McGee, and he is welcome to the fame of his work. The people of Santa Fe seem utterly destitute of taste."

Even the foreign traders had put up stores around the plaza that were far from pretty. An over-supply of saloons and gambling halls also gave offense. From the crowded interiors of the latter, one could hear the clack of rolling dice at the chuck-a-luck tables. "I cannot begin to catalogue all the vices of Santa Fe," intoned Rideing piously, "for it is probably the fastest little city in the world."

After rest and refreshment, he and his companions returned in the evening to find "quite an active throng circulating on the plaza—fashionably dressed civilians, military officers in blue and gold, teamsters with rawhide whips, and dashing cavalrymen with clanking spurs. There were even some tastefully dressed children afoot, with natty nursery maids in attendance. And we began to think better of Santa Fe."

After returning home, William Rideing collected his newspaper features and they were brought out by a New York book publisher in 1879 under the title, *A-Saddle in the Wild West*. To many of its readers, Santa Fe probably seemed like a foreign place, indeed.

A Bostonian visiting New Mexico in 1868 thought its adobe houses were unfit for habitation

A BOSTONIAN'S PREJUDICED VIEW OF NEW MEXICO

FOR MORE THAN 175 YEARS Easterners have been visiting New Mexico and sending back home a record of their impressions. Some found the unfamiliar land and people to be exotic and charming. But others, out of simple prejudice or self-righteousness, condemned everything in sight.

Among the latter was a Massachusetts man who saw the Territory soon after the Civil War and summarized his observations in a letter to the *Boston Evening Transcript*. It was published in the April 11, 1868 issue, a copy of which recently came into my hands.

The correspondent, as was often the custom in those days, did not sign his letter, but gave his initials instead: C.N.W. So his identity remains unknown. However, since the letter was posted from Fort Wingate, New Mexico, we can guess that he was a soldier, probably newly stationed in the Southwest.

Fort Wingate was located north of the Zuni Mountains, a few miles east of the future Gallup. It took its name from Captain Benjamin Wingate, who died of wounds received in the Battle of Valverde on the Rio Grande.

Traveling to and from the fort, our C.N.W. seems to have developed some strong opinions on the New Mexicans and their customs.

"The native inhabitants here," he said, "are all either wild Indians, tame Indians (Pueblos), or Mexicans. The first we do not cultivate as bosom friends, lest we end up in our grave, as a result of an Apache arrow."

Nor did the snooty Bostonian have much use for the remaining two categories of residents, whom he described as immoral and woefully ignorant. The Pueblo people, however, he found "rather more amusing" than the Mexicans.

"Our sources of amusement, besides human beings," continued he, "are donkeys, wolves, ravens, prairie dogs, and rattlesnakes. We can sit up all night, like Daniel, looking at a show of wild animals, and it needn't cost us a cent."

"Once in a while we hear that somebody has been shot in the Plaza at Santa Fe, or that the Navajos have murdered a few miserable shepherds and run off a few thousand sheep. But there the exciting news stops."

"Upon reaching us, our eastern newspapers are so old that their sensational headlines no longer electrify. We heard of President Andrew Johnson's impending impeachment with as little emotion as we would have felt on being told that Bismark had breakfasted on soft crabs."

In his litany of complaints, C.N.W. also took aim at the regional architecture, for which he had little use. He thought there was no way that houses made of earth and straw and devoid of landscaping could be made "pleasant to the eye," even with a thorough whitewashing.

"Some of our deluded correspondents, referring to New Mexican houses, have written of 'adobe palaces.' Let nobody imagine that a good Eastern barn isn't a more desirable habitation than any adobe residence in this boundless territory."

One day twenty Indians from Zuni Pueblo came plodding into Fort Wingate. Our Boston letter-writer and several companions went out to meet them, but decided that the natives looked more picturesque from a distance than they did on closer view. "Their clothes were filthy and we were obliged to shake 20 dirty hands," was the cutting comment.

"One old Indian," mused C.N.W., "was looked upon as a prodigy in English, because he had learned somewhere to say, 'How do doo?' which he repeated on the slightest provocation."

"Though the Zunis are the oldest Catholics in this country, they were induced by a bribe of tobacco to give us a war dance even though it was during Lent. From their dance gestures we judged it to be a recital of a battle scene with their enemies, the Navajos."

Being a rigid Yankee with firm ideas of industry and thrift, C.N.W. spoke approvingly of the small numbers of Americans who had settled in New Mexico. Their aim was to reap a fortune from the god-forsaken country.

Newcomers who were ambitious and sharp, he concluded, should have no trouble in turning natural resources and local products into money. "But it will take a powerful agent," he said in parting, "to break the apathy of the native people whom hundreds of years have failed to push even a step forward towards civilization."

We can only imagine what Boston readers of the *Evening Transcript* must have thought of New Mexico upon digesting the heavy-handed letter from Fort Wingate.

VIII

WOMEN OF GUMPTION

The Lady in Blue (17th century woodcut)

MYSTERY OF THE BLUE LADY

TO MY MIND one of the most enchanting stories of the Spanish Southwest deals with the miraculous flights of Mother María de Agreda who visited the Indians of New Mexico and Texas in the 1620s. A history-minded friend of mine even went so far as to name his daughter Agreda, after the famous nun.

She was born in 1602 in the castle of a noble family on the border between the Spanish kingdoms of Aragon and Navarre. It was said that her mother experienced no pain at childbirth, and thus knew at once that María was predestined to work for the glory of God.

At the age of twelve the girl became a nun. So great was her piety that she began to experience constant visions and revelations. One day while in a trance, María felt herself transported to America where God commanded her to preach to the Indians.

The native people of New Mexico and surrounding provinces had proven especially resistant to conversion, so she was ordered to concentrate her attention on them. Even though she used Spanish, they understood her as distinctly as if she spoke their Indian language.

The tribesmen were astonished by her appearance, not knowing who she was or where she came from. Since she wore a bright blue cloak over the shoulders, they called her simply the "Lady in Blue."

Over the next decade María "bi-located" or made 500 flights to New Mexico and Texas. In 1627 she became the abbess of her convent, by which time her extraordinary journeys had become well known.

In the first place, she had told the priest, who was her spiritual guide, about them and because of the details she could provide, he believed her.

And then secondly, the missionaries of New Mexico began getting reports from the Indians about a strange lady who came among them to give religious instruction.

One day Father Alonso de Benavides, head of the Franciscan Order in New Mexico, was sitting in the shade at the old Isleta Mission on the Rio Grande. Looking east, he saw a group of 50 strange Indians approaching across the plain.

The priest of Isleta told him that these were Jumanos from central Texas and that they came every year asking for missionaries. When the party arrived, Father Benavides invited them inside the church compound and then began to quiz their leaders.

Yes, they were Jumanos and they had come on a long journey bearing an urgent request. Missionaries must be sent to their villages. Why? Because a Lady in Blue had converted them and told them to travel to New Mexico and make this demand.

Benavides was not as astonished as he might have been because he was well-acquainted with the stories circulating in his native Spain concerning María de Agreda and her claims of bi-location. In fact he carried special instructions to investigate the matter at the New Mexico end and send a report to both the King and the Pope.

With the returning Jumanos, Benavides sent two missionaries who went as far as their villages on the Conchos River near modern San Angelo. On their arrival the whole tribe came out carrying two large crosses. When asked who wanted baptism, all raised their hands. And all seemed to know their catechism. The Lady in Blue had done her work with thoroughness.

Eight years later Father Benavides left New Mexico and returned to Spain. One of the first things he did was visit the convent of María de Agreda.

In testing her, he asked questions about the landscape and the customs of the Indians that only someone who had actually been in New Mexico could know. In his report, he recorded, "She convinced me absolutely by describing to me all the things along the Rio Grande as I have seen them myself, as well as by other details which I shall keep within my soul."

As further proof the nun mentioned that she had distributed little crosses and rosaries to the Indians. Benavides remembered seeing these when first approached by the Jumanos.

In 1631, María de Agreda, according to her own statement was released by God from her obligation of bi-locating and preaching in America. She lived a quiet, pious life in her convent for another 30 years. Even today there is some sentiment among the faithful to elevate her to sainthood.

Anyone who reads regularly in the chronicles of Southwestern history will find from time to time references by Spanish conquistadors, wandering missionaries, and French explorers to the widely-traveled Lady in Blue. According to one enthusiastic church scholar, her story represents "a mystic phenomenon unparalleled in the history of the world."

That may be overstating the case just a bit. But the truth is, the tale is certainly unparalleled in the annals of colonial New Mexico.

Adobe walls and a defensive torreon, resembling those in the 18th century Villalpando hacienda

MRS. VILLALPANDO'S LAST STAND

IN THE SUMMER OF 1760, Don Pablo de Villalpando was counted as one of the richest and most prominent men in the Taos Valley. His huge flocks of sheep, under the watchful eye of herders, grazed the foothills and high meadows of the nearby Sangre de Cristo Mountains. His fields kept his storerooms bulging. And his spacious adobe house, resembling a medieval fortress, was judged a marvel by all who saw it.

Don Pablo's home had been built with an eye to sheltering not only his own family and workers, but also, in times of danger, his neighbors. It had high, thick walls, four round defensive towers at each corner and a stout wooden gate. Indian raiders, who swept through the valley on periodic forays, gave it a wide berth. They considered the ramparts unassailable.

During the first week of August, the master of this frontier estate departed upon a business trip. As was his custom, he left his wife in charge for she knew as well as he what steps to take in any emergency.

Scarcely had Don Pablo left when disturbing news reached the valley. The Comanches were on the rampage and an army of warriors, said to number 3000, was marching through the mountain pass on the east. They were bent upon attacking and destroying their old enemies, the Indians of Taos Pueblo, who lived a short distance beyond the Villalpando hacienda.

The alarm was sounded. The Spanish folk gathered up their children and hurried to find refuge behind the fortress gates. Señora Villalpando was there, distributing muskets to the men, fourteen in all, as they passed inside. The women were given lances to form a second line of defense.

Like a cloud of hornets, the painted and befeathered Comanches swarmed across the plain and approached the massive mud walls. Noisily, they put on an impressive display of horsemanship, dashing back and forth at breakneck speed and all the while brandishing their weapons. Likely they would have ridden on to their main objective, Taos Pueblo, as soon as the performance was completed and left the hacienda unmolested. But some of the Spaniards crowding the walls became unnerved by the spectacle and let go with their muskets. Instantly a full-scale battle erupted.

With blood-chilling war cries the Indians charged and encircled the building. In spite of heavy fire, many of them were able to reach the walls where they began chopping holes with their knives. The settlers above who leaned out trying to get a shot fell riddled with arrows. When small entrances had been hacked open, warriors poured through.

Inside they set fire to the place and grabbed up screaming children. Near the main gate Señora Villalpando, swinging her lance was the last defender still standing. In the midst of a bloody melee she finally fell.

The magnitude of the tragic encounter was overwhelming: the once-proud hacienda in ruins, all the men and many of the women slain, and 64 children and younger woman carried into captivity. Also 49 of the Comanches had died in the bitter fighting. Pablo de Villalpando returned home to find his family extinguished and his property devastated.

The war party carried its prisoners to camps far out on the Texas plains. The following summer a group of Comanche traders returned to Taos and brazenly offered seven of the captives for ransom. The Spanish governor in a fury attacked the Indians, killed many of them, and liberated the prisoners.

But what of the remainder who had been carried off at the time of the massacre? Several of the women, we know, were traded from one tribe to another, until years later they were rescued by frontiersmen from the East. Taken to St. Louis and New Orleans, they passed the remainder of their lives on the banks of the Mississippi.

About one of them, Maria Rosalia, the daughter of Pablo Villalpando, we have a few details. She was ransomed by a French trader Jean Baptiste Sale de Lajoie and conducted to St. Louis where the two were married by a priest. The couple had two daughters, one of whom married French merchant William Leroux. Their son Antoine Leroux later became a mountain man in New Mexico and took up part time residence with his Villalpando cousins at Taos.

Pablo Villalpando never learned the fate of daughter Maria Rosalia, but he would have been pleased if he could have known that her grandson would one day return to the Taos home of his ancestors.

Governor Lew Wallace, Husband of Susan Wallace

SUSAN WALLACE WRITES A BOOK

ON MAY 6, 1852 A STRUGGLING YOUNG LAWYER in Crawfordsville, Indiana named Lew Wallace married the town beauty, blue-eyed Susan Elston. Her wealthy father was not keen on the match, believing the groom showed little promise.

As it turned out, papa was wrong. Wallace had a dramatic and prosperous career, and his devoted wife Susan shared the triumphs and hardships with him.

In the Civil War, he rose quickly to the rank of major-general, the youngest man to reach that level in the Union Army. He played a key role in the battle of Shiloh and successfully defended Cincinnati from a Confederate invasion.

Active in politics, Wallace befriended and advised presidents from Lincoln through Teddy Roosevelt. A budding author and artist, he was half way through the writing of his novel *Ben-Hur* when President Rutherford B. Hayes appointed him territorial governor of New Mexico.

Wallace reached Santa Fe in late September, 1878, alone. Having heard that New Mexico was a wild and primitive place, he told Susan to wait in Indiana until he checked out living conditions there.

Early the next year, with a come-ahead from her husband, she bought a train ticket to the end of the line, then at Trinidad, Colorado. From that point, she was driven in an open buckboard two continuous days and nights to Santa Fe. The whole way, she huddled under a buffalo robe to keep warm.

Approaching the plaza at trail's end, her driver shouted, "La Fonda," and stopped before the hotel. "The drowsy old town," Susan thought, "looked older than the hills and worn-out besides."

Her first unfavorable impression was afterward confirmed. The squat cluster of adobe houses, she decided, resembled a brickyard. The streets were dirty, swarming with hungry dogs. And the dusky, weathered women went about "with dismal old black shawls over their heads."

Susan Wallace was haughty, spoiled, and unfamiliar with the ways of the world outside her native Indiana. But she was observant, and like her husband, an aspiring writer.

Upon setting foot in New Mexico, she began taking detailed notes. As much to relieve boredom as anything else, Mrs. Wallace used them to write up a series of articles for eastern periodicals.

In 1888, seven years after leaving New Mexico, her collected pieces were published in New York as a book, *The Land of the Pueblos*. Several illustrations, sketched by her husband in and around Santa Fe, were included in its pages.

Most notable was Lew Wallace's drawing of the old Palace of the Governors, as it appeared during his residency. Since its first publication, the image has been reproduced many times.

Susan in her writing was especially attentive to local customs. Wash day, for instance, fascinated her.

Women walked to the *acequias* or river with laundry in flat Indian baskets on their heads. In the water, they pounded dirty clothes with smooth stones, making "the buttons fly." Then they spread the wet laundry on the grass to dry, "as young Roman girls still do along the Tiber River," said the author.

The Governor in 1880 inspected southern New Mexico where Apaches were ravaging the countryside. He had an armed escort and Susan tagged along.

At a village above Socorro, the people turned out to welcome the Governor and his wife. They showed them sixteen mutilated bodies resting in the church, victims of a raid. The lady from Santa Fe was horrified.

Such incidents on this and other trips supplied Susan Wallace with plenty of material that ended up in *The Land of the Pueblos*. But her book, composed in stilted Victorian language, enjoyed only a modest success in its day.

The fate of Lew Wallace's book was quite different, however. Late in his term, a woman stopped him on the Santa Fe plaza and asked about it.

"I have just sent *Ben-Hur* off to the publisher," he replied. "Do you think I will get enough for it to pay the postage?"

Unexpectedly, his epic novel became a world-wide bestseller and ultimately a major Hollywood film. It easily paid for the original postage many times over.

Mrs. Stevenson confronts Zuni religious leaders
(*Police Gazette*, March 1886)

THE INDOMITABLE MRS. STEVENSON

IN 1879 THE NEWLY ORGANIZED Bureau of American Ethnology in Washington, D.C. sent an expedition to the Southwest. Its purpose was to carry out research among the Pueblo Indians and also acquire cultural artifacts for the Smithsonian Institution.

Heading this work was Colonel James Stevenson, a prominent geologist and self-taught anthropologist. Accompanying him as research assistant was his wife Matilda Coxe Stevenson, known to her friends as Tilly.

Bureau officials thought that she would prove useful in gathering information from Pueblo women that ordinarily would not be divulged to a man. So Tilly was allowed to go to Puebloland as an unpaid volunteer.

The expedition selected Zuni Pueblo as its base and the members remained there for six months. In that time, the Stevensons and their co-workers conducted numerous interviews, made archeological surveys in the area, and purchased or received as gifts some 3,000 Zuni artifacts.

The majority of these were pottery items, but every other category of Zuni material culture was represented in their collection. By the time the expedition left, we have to wonder whether a single old pot remained in the village.

For the next few years, the Stevensons annually returned to the region to continue their activities. Although they ranged from

Zia Pueblo (near Bernalillo) in the east to the Hopi towns on the west, the focus of their interest remained at Zuni.

Mrs. Stevenson's role as an interviewer grew in time and she also wrote up the reports from data collected by her husband. When he died from tick fever in 1888, the Bureau appointed her to the staff so that she could continue their work.

In 1904 the Government Printing Office published Matilda Coxe Stevenson's 607 page book entitled *The Zuni Indians*. The oversize volume weighs just under six pounds. Covering the culture as a whole, it gives largest emphasis to religion and ceremonies.

Tilly, however, had earned the reputation of being strong-willed and domineering. While in Washington, between research trips, she expected Bureau personnel to do her bidding and kept the office in turmoil.

The Pueblo Indians, too, found Tilly to be an intrusive and formidable woman. In her missionary zeal to record native customs before they disappeared, she made no apology for stepping on toes.

Once she confronted a Pueblo elder who had objected to her interference. A sensational picture showing Mrs. Stevenson, armed with an umbrella and shaking her fist in the Indian's face, was printed in the *Illustrated Police News*, an eastern tabloid.

On another occasion she forced her way into a restricted area during the planting of prayer plumes in the Shalako ceremony, one of Zuni's most sacred rites. An argument with the Pueblo governor ensued but Tilly stayed put.

In one instance, however, her meddling apparently saved a life. Mrs. Stevenson assembled and printed a great deal of information on witchcraft, which had a firm hold on the Zuni mind.

An informant of hers had long been accused of being a wizard. When a young woman died, he was blamed by the village council and condemned to be hanged. Mrs. Stevenson found him at home, sadly spending his last hours with his wife and daughter.

She persuaded the "wizard" to go with her to the council, still in session. There she made an impassioned speech, explaining that she had lifted the curse of witchcraft from his shoulders, so that he was no longer a danger to the community. The council believed firmly in Tilly's powers, and the sentence of execution was at once lifted.

Mrs. Stevenson's conduct in such episodes would not be tolerated now. And her big book on Zuni is today often dismissed as outdated. Yet, she preserved much valuable data that would have otherwise been lost.

The fact stands that Matilda Coxe Stevenson was the first woman ethnologist to work in the Southwest. For that alone, she deserves to be honored as a pioneer scholar.

One of the last New Mexico stagecoaches

THE REMARKABLE SADIE

SO FAR AS WE KNOW, the New Mexico Territory had only one female stagecoach driver. She was Sarah Jane Orchard, known to friend and foe alike as Sadie.

Born in England, Sadie performed on the London stage before leaving to seek her fortune in America around 1885. From New York, she made her way across country to the booming mining town of Kingston in central New Mexico.

There opportunities for women were limited. So Sadie opened the one business for which there was an unfulfilled demand: a "sporting house," as polite society archly termed places where women entertained gentlemen after dark.

In author Erna Fergusson's words, "Sadie was a tiny high-bosomed woman with small feet, tight spitcurls, and a wicked chuckle to punctuate her obscenities. All accounts agree that she was both tough and shrewd."

In spite of her rough edges, the little English woman wished to be accepted in the community. So she raised $1,500 to build the first church.

The structure went up and the opening services were held. Sadie and her "soiled doves" attended but were promptly snubbed by proper citizens. She never again entered the church.

As the mines declined in Kingston, Sadie moved to nearby Hillsboro and opened two hotels. She also married a timid man who owned the Lake Valley, Hillsboro & Kingston Stage line.

His coaches picked up mail and passengers at the Lake Valley railhead and transported them to the mining district beyond. After the wedding, Sadie took control of both his life and stage business.

The line owned two Concord coaches and an express wagon. Why Sadie on occasion chose to take bullwhip in hand and make the stage runs in place of the regular drivers is not altogether certain.

The excitement must have appealed to a person of her nature. And perhaps, being an upsetter of tradition, she wished to shock the public.

To date no one had ever seen a woman—and a small one at that—on the seat of a coach handling the reins of a four-horse team.

Sadie herself was never held up by bandits, but one of the other drivers, Bill Holt, was. A large sum of money was being shipped in a strong box and word had gotten around.

Just out of Hillsboro, Holt stopped the coach in a secluded grove of trees. Removing the cash from the box, he stuffed it inside the horsecollars on the team. Feeling more secure, he snapped the whip and continued on.

A few miles farther and masked men with drawn pistols halted the stage. They demanded money. Calmly, Bill Holt informed them that it had been carried through by Sadie Orchard on the previous day's run.

The thieves searched the coach and found nothing. Spurring away in a cloud of dust, they cursed their ill luck. The driver reached Lake Valley and delivered his strong box intact to the railroad agent.

Sadie was so pleased with the outcome that she presented Holt with a $100 reward. Years later she claimed that it was her idea to hide the money in the horsecollars.

The ship of marriage for Sadie eventually was wrecked upon the reefs of discord. Her husband, henpecked beyond endurance, took to drink. In 1902 he lost the mail contract, and then the stageline to bankruptcy. The fellow left town for good.

Single once again, Sadie went back to operating a bordello. When the terrible influenza of 1917 struck, she nursed the sick, cared for new-made orphans, and helped pay funeral expenses for families too poor to bury their dead.

As the mines played out and Hillsboro began to wither, Sadie Orchard lingered on, a fading relic of the past. When she died in the early 1940s at almost 90 years of age, her money was gone and her old friends long dead.

Scarcely anyone recalled then that she had done her part on the New Mexico frontier, driving stagecoaches and performing acts of charity. In spite of faults, she had carved her own small niche in history.

The Museum of New Mexico owns one of the Concord coaches that Sadie drove long ago. Tiny Hillsboro, on the east slope of the Black Range, can be visited today. Walk the tree-lined main street and you'll be treading in the footsteps of the unconventional Sadie Orchard.

Comanche Warriors (Addison photo, Museum of New Mexico)

RACHAEL PLUMMER'S CAPTIVITY

IN THE ANNALS OF WESTWARD EXPANSION, there exists a body of literature known as captive narratives. It is comprised of accounts by people who were captured by Indians and later escaped or were ransomed.

On the whole, such narratives make grim reading and should not be pursued by those with weak stomachs. But they do serve to convey a vivid picture of the realities of the frontier experience.

Most of the stories were from women and children, since adult men almost never survived Indian captivity. What happened to them, General Nelson A. Miles said in his memoirs, "was simply too shocking and horrible to write out in words."

On the southern plains, the Comanche warrior was considered a pure genius when it came to inventing new methods of torture. That was according to General Richard Irving Dodge who knew the tribe well.

Confirming his observation was the story of Rachael Plummer, a young pregnant woman seized by a Comanche war party in 1836 during their massacre at Fort Parker, Texas.

Taken with her was her two year old son James and her cousin Cynthia Ann Parker, who would remain with the tribe many years and give birth to the last Comanche war chief, the celebrated Quanah Parker.

Rachael would remain with her captors for 21 months as a virtual slave before her ransoming. On the party's initial flight into New Mexico, she was regularly beaten, once left semi-conscious on the ground.

Later she wrote, "While nearly smothering in my own blood I could hear my little James crying for mother and hear the blows they gave him and his weakened voice. I leave you to reflect what were my feelings."

Then she adds, "They took him away and that was the last sight I ever had of my little James."

Months later in the Comanche camp she bore a second son, naming him Luther Plummer after his slain father, "a beautiful babe" in her words.

When it was six weeks old, the Comanches snatched the infant from her arms and tortured it to death in front of her eyes.

Of her child, Rachael said, "After it was torn to pieces one of them held it by a leg, brought the body to me and threw it in my lap."

She concludes, "In praise to the savages, I must say they gave me time to dig a small hole in the earth and deposit it away. I was truly glad that it was entirely over its sufferings."

Finally, some native New Mexicans, who had friendly passage, entered the tipi camp and began to negotiate for Mrs. Plummer's release.

In fact, they were acting on behalf of William Donoho, a hotel keeper in Santa Fe, who had heard of her plight and had gotten together a quantity of goods as a ransom.

Rachael had remembered that the traders from New Mexico "made an offer for me which my owners refused, but at length they succeeded in buying me. Oh joy that mortal tongue can never tell."

The poor woman was swiftly conveyed to Santa Fe and showered with kindness by Donoho and his wife Mary. Historian Marian Meyer has written a book on the Donohos, telling of their role in saving Rachael Plummer.

Soon all three went to Missouri on the Santa Fe Trail, and a compassionate William Donoho escorted Mrs. Plummer to surviving relatives in Texas.

Rachael recorded her terrible experiences in a little book published in Houston in 1838. Only one copy of that original edition survives, but a number of expanded editions appeared later.

She died on February 19, 1839, a little over a year after her liberation. The physical cruelties suffered in captivity were the direct cause of her premature death.

In her last days, she grieved for her little James whom she assumed had perished. But four years after her passing, he was discovered alive among the Comanches and rescued.

Sometime ago I received a letter from an 83 year old Plummer family descendant, asking how she could find a copy of Rachael's narrative.

I sent her one and she replied, saying how painful it was to read of that horrible ordeal. But still, the lady noted, "I was glad to learn about this chapter in my family history."

Otero Optic, June 5, 1879

"STEAMBOAT" AT OTERO

MY FRIEND, GENEALOGIST LOUIS F. SERNA of Albuquerque, prints a dandy little periodical, "The Sernas of New Mexico Newsletter," about family history. In it recently he said a few words concerning the short-lived town of Otero and one of its more eccentric citizens, a dancehall maiden known as "Steamboat."

The name of the place I knew, because it was home to one of the New Mexico Territory's best newspapers, the *Otero Optic*. But the lady called Steamboat, I had somehow missed.

Eagerly, I plunged into my large personal library of New Mexico books to learn more about the town and also find out what I could about Madam Steamboat. My quest led, not unexpectedly, to Miguel A. Otero, Jr. The first volume of his memoirs contained information on both.

Miguel's father had long been a power in territorial business and politics. In the late 1870s, he was a senior partner in the firm of Otero, Seller & Co., a commission house that engaged in wholesaling and retailing, while freighting its wares from Kansas railheads to customers in New Mexico.

As the Atchison, Topeka & Santa Fe Railway slowly pushed its track across southeastern Colorado, Otero, Seller & Co. moved its commission house and all employees to each new railhead.

Miguel Otero, Sr. became the railroad's agent and obtained a right-of-way through New Mexico, along with concessions from the legislature at Santa Fe.

In gratitude, the AT&SF made him one of its directors and when the first steel rail was laid inside New Mexico, he was selected to drive a golden spike.

Further, Miguel Jr. declared, "In recognition of the part my father played in this development, the first railroad town and station in New Mexico was named Otero." It was located on the flats about five miles outside the southern entrance to Raton Pass.

The late T.M. Pearce once wrote that Otero became "a lively spot," an understatement at best. Railroad workers and saloons moved in, as several commission houses went up. From the start, the community showed a wild and lawless side.

According to Louis Serna, one of the denizens of the camp was a busy madam who tipped the scales at 350 plus pounds. He says her name was Dolores Martínez and she ran a dancehall and venue of pleasures of the evening. Because of her gargantuan size, she was affectionately known up and down the line as "Steamboat."

Miguel Jr. at age eighteen went to work as a clerk in his father's office at Otero. He claims that Steamboat, a native of Mora, opened her first pleasure palace at the railhead of Hays City, Kansas in 1868. Then, as tracks were laid southwest, she followed each new camp into New Mexico.

Her dancehall in Otero attracted "all the tough characters on the border." Gun play was common among the trigger-happy customers.

One evening a drunk cowboy began shooting up the packed hall. Steamboat was creased by a bullet and "fell backward with a crashing thump on the floor." Carried by many hands to the doctor's office next door, she got patched up and was back to work an hour later.

Scarcely a year passed from Otero's founding before the AT&SF reached Las Vegas, on July 4, 1879. The railroad gangs moved there to begin work on track pointing toward Santa Fe. The commission houses and Steamboat followed them.

So did Russell Kistler, editor of the *Optic*. He took his press and newspaper to Las Vegas and became embroiled in politics. The *Las Vegas Optic* publishes to this day.

As for Madam Steamboat, Miguel Jr. tells us that after Las Vegas, she went home to Mora, taking a tidy sum saved over the years. It was quite enough to keep her comfortably fixed for the remainder of her life. "She deserves a page in the history of the old frontier," he recalled long afterward.

Miguel A. Otero, Jr. was destined to have his own story written there. He served two terms as territorial governor of New Mexico, 1897-1906. By all accounts, he was among the most able and progressive men who held that office.

Geronimo on horseback (left) with his warriors
(Smithsonian Institution photograph)

FLEEING FROM GERONIMO

THE FINAL SURRENDER of Apache war leader Geronimo in 1886 was hailed by journalists at the time as a momentous event. The old warhorse had caused such havoc and slain so many people that the populations of both New Mexico and Arizona heaved a collective sigh of relief.

For a generation, people who had lived through the Geronimo raiding era repeated stories of their own experiences. One of those was Nellie Brown who wrote down her recollections.

In 1885, while still a young woman, Nellie resided with her parents and two older brothers on their Double Springs Ranch in the rough country of west-central New Mexico. The family was 80 miles from a post office and 15 miles from the nearest neighbors at the N-Bar Ranch.

While the men worked the cattle, young Nellie helped her mother with household chores. Free times she saddled her mustang pony and went riding. Always she carried a pearl-handled Smith and Wesson six-shooter.

Early one morning a rider dashed up to the ranch house. Brother Fred went out to hear whatever urgent news was brought. He returned on the run and announced, "Apaches are coming this way and we must get out of here."

As Nellie later described it, "We got up in a hurry, but our faces were white and our hands trembled as we dressed." Her father went right out with an axe and chopped the rooster's head off, so he wouldn't crow and attract the attention of any passing Indian.

Nearby was a ruined fort and the entire family went there, carrying guns and provisions. They remained inside, in hiding, for two days.

Then a pair of cowboys with a small herd of cattle passed by. They said the rumor of Geronimo and his Apaches being off the reservation was unfounded. "We believed the cowboy's story," related Nellie, "so we returned home and the men went back to work."

After a bit Fred saddled up a horse and set out for the mining town of Kingston to pick up the mail. He had been gone a day and a half when suddenly the ranch house was confronted by 30 men on panting horses.

Fred had met this citizens' posse on the trail to Kingston. The riders said they were glad to see him alive for Geronimo was on the warpath after all. They had been heading for the Double Spring Ranch to see whether anyone survived.

When Fred found his family safe, he broke down in tears. Said Nellie, "He told us of the deeds of murder, bloodshed and pillage that Geronimo had committed. We were almost the last settlers who had not left the country for places of safety in the towns.

Nellie's father locked the front door and nailed a sign to it that read, "Look Out for Indians." That was to warn any lone cowboy or prospector passing through.

The family climbed in a buckboard and started out, with the posse riding guard ahead and behind. Five miles down the road, they found moccasin tracks at a spring.

The next day the little cavalcade passed a cabin and found the owner dead in his yard. A grandfather clock had been dragged from the house and torn apart.

Later there were reports of an Apache warrior who wore a string of clock wheels for earrings. That little detail became part of the pioneer lore of southwestern New Mexico.

As the party threaded its way through Corduroy Canyon, a shot was heard ahead where one of the men had gone scouting. Believing it was an ambush, the men lashed their horses into a run.

Nellie drew out her six-shooter and cocked it. Afterward she remembered that her only thought had been at that moment, "I'm in for it, I'll fight, but I'll die game—like an American girl." Believe it or not, people on the frontier really did think in terms like that.

As it turned out, there was no ambush. The scout's rifle had accidentally discharged. In a few hours all were safe in town and enjoying the hospitality settlers extended to one another in hours of crises.

In commenting upon the fearsome episode, Nellie declared, "I have always been thankful that my scalp never came to rest as an ornament on Geronimo's belt. I heard that red was his favorite color, and my hair was a lively curly red."

IX

THROUGH CHILDREN'S EYES

Territorial family dressed up for a formal portrait

GROWING UP IN NEW MEXICO

A CHILDHOOD SPENT on the Southwestern frontier often lingered in memory as a harsh, bitter experience. Life for youngsters in those days was filled with abundant danger, lots of hard work, a poor diet, and few comforts.

Still, even under the bleakest circumstances children managed to admit a little light and amuse themselves at play. It has been that way since time began.

If we could return to the 19th century and visit plazas and town squares along the Rio Grande, we would find them filled with young people running, shouting, kicking a ball, or playing tag while chanting:

"Chase the Devil around the stump,
And give him a kick at every jump."

Marion Russell who came to New Mexico by wagon train as a child of seven in 1852 remembered that she and her little brother made a game of gathering buffalo chips (dried dung) for the campfire.

Under the chips they found holes in the ground where tarantulas lived. "When we found such a hole," said Marion, "we would stomp on the earth beside it and sing, 'Tarantula, tarantula! Come out. Come out. Tell us what it is all about.'

"And sure enough they would come out walking on long stilt-like legs. As a reward for having obeyed we would squash them."

A visitor to Acoma Pueblo in the 1880s got a glimpse of Indian youngsters having a good time. He says, "In front of the adobe houses were groups of children, playing in little patches of sand, or tossing pebbles at a mark.

"The children of Acoma never saw a doll nor any other manufactured plaything. They amuse themselves with sticks, stones and mud pies, having a great deal better time than many white children."

And something else this traveler noticed: "These small Indians hardly ever cry. In the time I have been among them, I have never seen them quarrel either, which is more than I can say for American boys and girls."

Pueblo children had various games played with bow and arrow, another in which a stone disc was thrown at upright corncobs in a circle, and then there was shinny. A team game like hockey, shinny was played in the village plaza with a ball and curved juniper sticks.

Spinning tops were carved by Pueblo boys from piñon wood and a buckskin string was used to turn them. Indian traders seem to have introduced the first tops, along with jumping jacks and marbles. Eastern merchants occasionally imported dolls, although local ones of cornhusks or rags were not unknown.

Before the turn of the last century, a New England scholar visited a hacienda in central New Mexico. "In the evening," he wrote, "we gathered by the light of the adobe fireplace and sang sweet Spanish folk-songs or played simple games.

"We played, for instance, 'Florón,' which is very much like 'Button, button, who's got the Button?' except that a ring is passed from hand to hand. A pretty Spanish couplet is sung throughout the game."

Other games popular in the Hispanic communities were *pitarilla, cañute, el coyotito,* and *las cazuelejas.* Adults played *cañute* (a guessing game) and gambled large sums of money.

When young Susan Magoffin entered New Mexico in 1846, she discovered that children swarmed around her like bees, out of curiosity. She was impressed by their manners and natural dignity, even barefoot six-year-olds making a formal bow.

Children on this frontier had to grow up quickly and assume adult responsibilities. Boys in their early teens fought Indians, and brides of thirteen and fourteen were not uncommon.

Just as soon as traveling photographers or studios appeared, beginning in the 1860s, parents had formal portraits taken of their offspring, to capture forever the fleeting image of childhood.

During the sentimental Victorian era, both boys and girls were dressed in frilly clothes and were photographed in stiff, unnatural poses. It was as if the artificiality of the scrubbed images was meant to hide the long history of hardship experienced by the majority of children.

William Carson, eldest son of Kit Carson (After E. Sabin)

KIT'S SON GOES TO COLLEGE

IN 1843 KIT CARSON MARRIED Josepha Jaramillo of Taos by whom he had seven children. The last, a girl, was born just one month before his death in May, 1868 at Fort Lyon, Colorado Territory.

Kit's eldest son was William, born in 1852. He may have named the boy after his grandfather or a half brother, both of whom were Williams. Or he may have been honoring his friend William Bent, one of the founders of Bent's Fort.

At age six little William was placed in the Lux Academy at Taos, a private school run by teacher John T. Lux. How long he attended is unknown, but while there he was commended for good conduct.

Kit was moving around a good deal in these years and the education of all his small children suffered. That fact was discovered by General William T. Sherman when he reached Fort Garland, Colorado where Kit was commander in 1866.

Sherman was holding a peace council with the Utes and Carson, who spoke half a dozen Indian languages, was serving as interpreter. During the meeting, his unruly nippers, scantily clad, bounced around the council room and disrupted the negotiations.

Dismayed, the General referred to them in his journal as "wild and untrained as a band of mustangs." And he turned to his host and remarked, "Kit, what are you doing about your children?"

The old scout replied that he feared his young were growing up uneducated and he felt that he had not done right by them. Clearly, he was concerned about the problem.

Kindly, Sherman told him that the Catholic College in Indiana (now Notre Dame) had recently given him a scholarship to bestow on a worthy boy and he would be glad to give it to William when he was old enough. Kit said thanks and he would keep it in mind.

Two years later as he was dying, he asked relatives to ship William back east to General Sherman who had promised to educate him. That was not quite what the General had said, of course.

Not long afterward, Sherman responded to a knock at the door of his St. Louis home. Outside stood a strapping 16-year-old William Carson with suitcase in hand. His possessions were simple: a pistol, a one volume biography of his late father, and $40 in cash.

"I am here to go to school," announced William. The General was startled and he had to think a moment to recall his offer to Kit. It had not included assuming full responsibility for the boy and his education.

But Sherman did his duty and packed William off to South Bend, Indiana to begin his studies. The scholarship only covered tuition, so he had to pay all other living expenses. The sum came to $300 the first year.

The new student lost no time in writing his benefactor for funds. In a painful scrawl his letter read, "Please tell me where shal I gate some money. I dont recollect where dead you tell me to geat some."

"My God," groaned the General, when he saw that. "The boy can't spell." Evidently, the Lux Academy back in Taos had not prepared its pupils for college.

William struggled through three years at the Catholic College, then flunked out. It was stated that he had "no appetite for learning."

Sherman, still shouldering his responsibility, next sent the boy to Fort Leavenworth, Kansas. He hoped he could learn enough to win a commission in the army. Lieutenant George Baird became his instructor.

Shortly, Baird wrote Sherman that young William "is very dull in all matters relating to books" owing to his poor education early in life. The Lieutenant said flatly that the boy could never pass the officer's test. In fact, he later failed it.

With that, the General gave up, having invested $1000 in trying to educate Kit's son. He declared, "By nature William was not adapted to modern uses."

Dejected, the youth returned to Colorado. There he took up ranching, a pursuit more in keeping with his nature, it would seem. He married a daughter of Tom Tobin, one of Kit's old companions.

Only one other fact of note remains to be told of the unlearned William. In 1889 he was unharnessing a plow horse and the animal kicked him.

The blow caused the pistol he was wearing in a holster to discharge. The bullet inflicted a fatal wound.

A Rocky Mountain newspaper proclaimed, "William Carson was shot by his horse last Friday." Kit's eldest son was 37 when he died.

Crushing Mill and Reduction Works, Southern New Mexico (After W.G. Ritch)

A BOY'S VIEW OF LIFE IN THE MINES

LITTLE JIM HASTINGS' FATHER was a mining man, so in 1880 when he lost his job in Colorado, he applied for another down in the New Mexico Territory. Offered the superintendency of a quartz mill crushing silver ore at Silver City, he set south alone with instructions for his family to follow when he had arranged a home.

Several weeks later the call came and Jim, with his mother and two sisters, took the newly built railroad over Raton Pass and rode as far as Albuquerque where the tracks ended. There they boarded a stagecoach for the last leg of the journey.

Sixty years afterward Jim could still recall the vivid scenes on that ride. "I remember seeing a Mexican plowing in the river bottom near Fort Craig with a pair of tiny oxen and a forked stick for a plow. We had no Indian trouble although they passed near us one night."

"We crossed the waterless desert called the Jornada del Muerto where the stage stations were every 20 miles or so. One we stopped at had a high adobe wall surrounding it and water hauled from the distant Rio Grande was always kept for travelers. The owner, a woman, maintained the station."

On May 1 the family arrived in Silver City and were met by Mr. Hastings who took them to their new home at the mill several miles from town. The mill operated 24 hours a day, 7 days a week crushing ore, so there was action aplenty to excite a young boy.

Jim watched the huge stamps that rose and fell hour after hour until the silver ore was pounded to dust. Washed in giant pans, it was ground again and then quicksilver was added to pick up the valuable metal. Evenings, Mr. Hastings loaded the day's recovery of silver into a wheelbarrow and pushed it to his home for safe-keeping. Little Jim walked by his side carrying a Colt revolver. In case of a hold-up, the boy had instructions to toss the pistol to his father and hit the dirt.

After enough of the silver accumulated, it was cast into large bricks weighing 300 pounds. Explained Jim, "These were unwieldy and much smaller ones would have been more convenient, but also more easily stolen."

When each brick was ready, it was consigned to the Wells Fargo Express Company whose Concord coach would carry it to the railroad in Deming. Once one of the heavy bricks fell through the floor when the coach hit a bump. The driver, unable to lift it, had to leave the $5,000 block of silver sitting in the middle of the desert road. But he knew it was safe. No pack mule could carry it away and had it been stolen in a wagon, any fast-riding posse could have easily caught up with the thief.

During the early 1880s the Apaches were still a menace in southwestern New Mexico. Jim never forgot the horror they inspired. When they were raiding, freighters refused to deliver food to the mill. Days at a time the Hastings and the workers had nothing to eat but corn bread and "sack pudding," that is, straight flour mush with no sugar.

The saddest sight he ever saw, Jim claimed, was one morning when two troopers from Fort Cummings brought in the wreck of a stagecoach. It was filled with bullet holes and covered with human blood. Everyone on board had died in an ambush.

The Indians had taken the stage horses and torn out every scrap of leather from the coach, to patch their moccasins and such. They had emptied the mail inside before making off with the express sacks. Letters delivered the next day to Silver City residents were decorated with blood stains.

Most days at the mill, however, were uneventful and young Jim found time to get to know the odd assortment of people who had collected there. He especially liked a colorful group of Chinese who rented land along a nearby stream and put in a truck garden.

"The first season they had it," he relates, "they carried their produce to market in baskets hung from yokes over their shoulders. They made a picturesque sight in their conical hats as they went along in single file, sing-songing to each other like a lot of blackbirds. The next season, they got a decrepit horse and an old market wagon, so that one man could sell the stuff and leave the rest at home to work."

For fun Jim one day hitched a ride on an ore wagon loaded with several tons of rock. Suddenly the wagon hit a stone and the boy was thrown off and under the rear wheel. Instantly, the driver yelled at his well-trained mules and they stopped dead in their tracks. Another few inches and Jim would have needed an undertaker.

As it was, he sprained both wrists in the fall. The only liniment in camp was for animals, a dark brown remedy. So that was liberally applied, and Jim declared that for a long while he was as dark as a Malay from Asia.

Reflecting back in his twilight years, Jim Hastings remembered his boyhood at the Silver City mill as a grand adventure. "As a youth, I was permitted to see the nation growing. No one dreamed in that faraway day of the stature it has now attained."

Silver City sheriff Harvey Whitehill,
who arrested twelve year old Billy for theft

BILLY'S BOYHOOD

BILLY THE KID HAD A SHORT LIFE! He was only twenty-one when Sheriff Pat Garrett shot him dead at Fort Sumner, New Mexico on July 14, 1881. All of the events that made him famous were crowded into the three years preceding his death.

The boyhood of Billy the Kid, therefore, formed a major part of his life. For most of it, we have only fragmentary information, and some episodes of his youth are mired in controversy.

Some twenty years ago I was invited to Silver City to speak at the dedication of a new state historical marker for the local Pioneer Cemetery. The most noted person buried there, I observed at the time, was Catherine Antrim, Billy's mother. She had died of tuberculosis in 1874 when he was fifteen.

The older histories acknowledged that Billy had spent his teens in Silver City, but they were fuzzy about how he got there and where he had been born. Historians have recently filled in a few of the pieces.

We now believe that Billy was born in the Irish slums of New York City, at 210 Greene Street, to be specific. He was christened Henry McCarty at the nearby Church of St. Peter.

About 1864 Billy's father died, and his mother Catherine took him and his older brother Joe to Indiana. There she established a relationship with one William H. Antrim who was thirteen years her junior.

Together, they all moved to Wichita, Kansas about 1870 where Antrim tried his hand at farming and Catherine McCarty took in laundry. By 1871, they had gone to Denver and two years later popped up in Santa Fe.

There on March 1, 1873 Catherine McCarty finally made things legal, by marrying William Antrim at the First Presbyterian Church. Her two young sons stood up as witnesses.

Almost immediately, the family headed down to Silver City. They may have decided that the climate in that corner of the Territory could benefit Catherine, who suffered from an advanced case of tuberculosis.

They settled into a log house at the end of Main Street, and Antrim began odd-jobbing and perhaps doing a little prospecting. His youngest step-son, Henry McCarty, was now being called Henry Antrim.

For reasons not clear, a few folks referred to him as Billy Antrim, the name of his step-father. Later, others would call him Kid Antrim. And eventually out of all of this came the coining of the moniker Billy the Kid, perhaps the most celebrated outlaw name in the annals of the Old West.

Billy, it seems, always looked younger than his true age. Hence, the nickname Kid. One of his childhood chums, Anthony Conner, said years later that Billy was "really girlish looking."

In fact, there is some reason to believe that when several Silver City schoolboys appeared in a stage production at Morrill's Opera House, young Billy Antrim (formerly Henry McCarty) played the part of a girl.

Several of Conner's other recollections of the future outlaw are revealing. "In those days, Billy was one of the best boys in town," he said. "He was very slender, weighed over 75 pounds, and had coal black hair and eyes."

"He got to be quite a reader, too. He was always sprawled out somewhere reading a book, when he wasn't working at Knight's Butcher Shop. Finally he took to reading the *Police Gazette* and dime novels."

That Billy cut his teeth on the *Police Gazette*, which featured crime stories, is certainly curious since he himself would make his mark on history as a criminal. Then of course, within twenty years, Billy the Kid would be a recurring figure in dime novels, the trashy literature consumed by the masses.

On the whole, however, the boy's youth seems to have been pretty tame and those who actually knew him then would claim afterward that he had been well behaved. The popular story, occasionally still heard today, that Billy had gunned down a man who insulted his mother, is pure fiction—part of the legend fabricated by dime novelists and others.

It was after Mrs. Antrim died in 1874 that her son, without her restraining hand, started to go astray. Billy's step-father gave him little attention and the boy engaged in some petty thefts.

At one point, he and a pal stole a basket of clothes from a Chinese laundry, mainly as a prank. But easy-going Sheriff Harvey Whitehill thought Kid Antrim needed to be taught a lesson, so he jailed him.

Anthony Conner believed the sheriff merely wished Billy to understand where such conduct might lead. Instead, the boy made a daring escape by climbing up the jailhouse chimney.

He fled to Arizona Territory where in 1877 he killed near Camp Grant his first man, a blacksmith who bullied him. From there, Billy the Kid made his way to New Mexico's Lincoln County to keep a date with his destiny.

A young Billy the Kid
(New Mexico Department of Development photograph)

www.ingramcontent.com/pod-product-compliance
Lightning Source LLC
Chambersburg PA
CBHW030137170426
43199CB00008B/100